WIRING
Home Networks

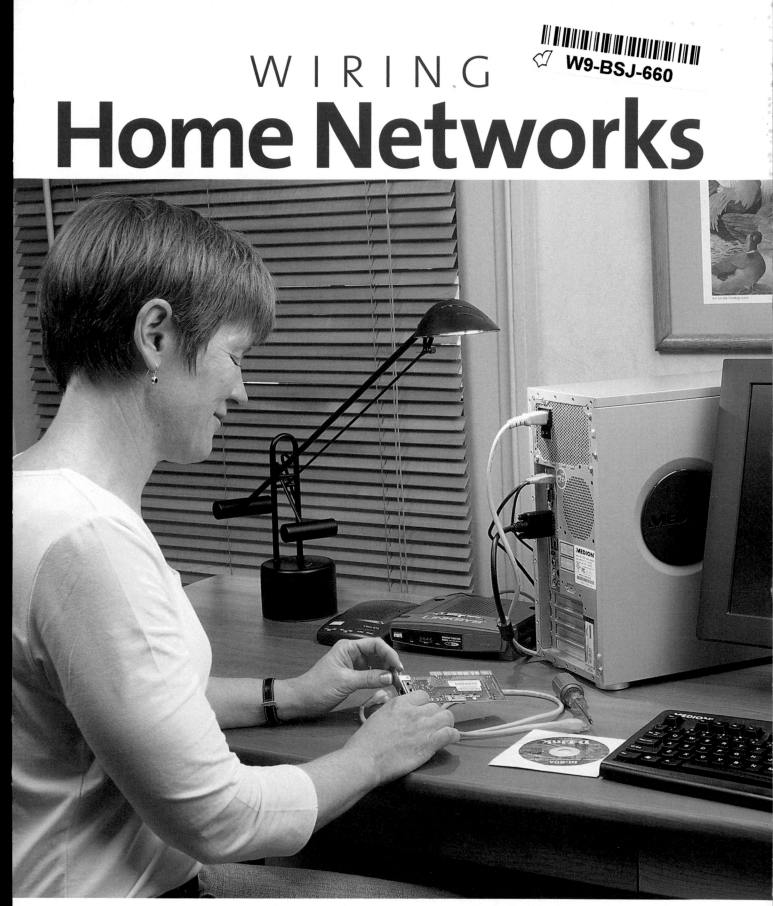

by John Ross and the Editors of Sunset Books
Menlo Park, California

SUNSET BOOKS

VICE PRESIDENT AND GENERAL MANAGER: Richard A. Smeby
VICE PRESIDENT AND EDITORIAL DIRECTOR: Bob Doyle
PRODUCTION DIRECTOR: Lory Day
OPERATIONS DIRECTOR: Rosann Sutherland
RETAIL SALES DEVELOPMENT MANAGER: Linda Barker
EXECUTIVE EDITOR: Bridget Biscotti Bradley
ART DIRECTOR: Vasken Guiragossian
SPECIAL SALES: Brad Moses

STAFF FOR THIS BOOK:
MANAGING EDITOR: Dave Toht
WRITER: John Ross
DESIGN: Rebecca Anderson
DESIGN ASSISTANT: Sarah Tibbot
PRINCIPAL PHOTOGRAPHER: Dan Stultz
ILLUSTRATOR: Steve Sanford
COPY EDITOR: Barbara McIntosh Webb
PROOFREADER: John Edmonds
INDEXER: Mary Pelletier Hunyadi

Additional photography: AT&T 35 TL; AVTech 11 B (inset); Belden Electronics Division 50; Cameron/Corbis 15; DirectTV 14, 25; Neema Frederick/Corbis Sygma 10 T; Howard Huang/The Image Bank 8; Jiang Jin/SuperStock 13; Linksys: 23, 27, 35 T; Andrew McKinney 37 B; Mealtime Pilot Initiative 12; Panasonic 35 TR; Plateau Corporation 31 T; Pulse Engineering Inc. (Excelsus) 57; Siemens 13 (silhouette), 33 B; SpeakerCraft 37 T and R; © 2000 TiVo Inc. All Rights Reserved 10 B; David Young-Wolff/Getty Images 11 T. Cover: Jamie Hadley (top row, middle); all others by Dan Stultz.

Special thanks to D-link Systems, Inc., Gateway, Inc., Ikea, Leviton Voice and Data Division, and MCC Technology Micro Computer Centers, Inc.

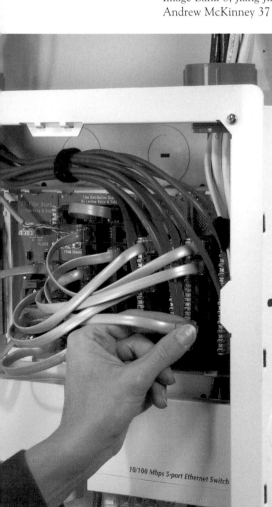

10 9 8 7 6 5 4 3 2 1

First printing June, 2004
Copyright © 2004
Sunset Publishing Corporation,
Menlo Park, CA 94025.

ISBN: 0-376-01806-2
Library of Congress Control Number: 2004105005
Printed in the United States.

For additional copies of *Wiring Home Networks* or any other Sunset book, call 1-800-526-5111. You can also visit us at www.sunset.com.

10/100 Mbps 5-port Ethernet Switch

CONTENTS

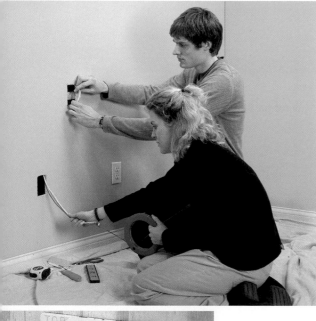

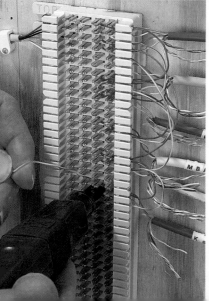

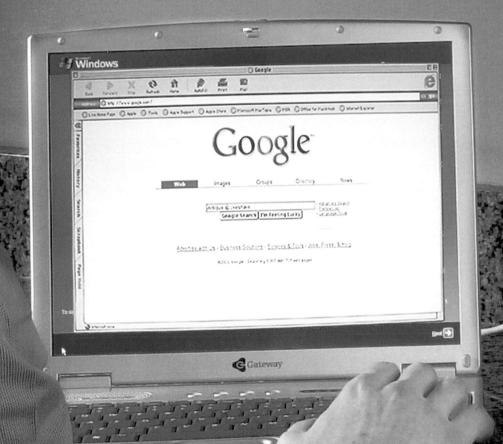

Perhaps what started you thinking about a network was a simple hankering to plug into the Internet from any room in the house— even the kitchen. However, a network can provide a wide variety of interconnections involving phone, data, video, and audio lines.

what kind of network is right for you?

MORE THAN EVER BEFORE, WE LIVE IN A WIRED WORLD. Today, household computers, the Internet, telephones, cable and satellite TV, and other services connect our homes to the wider world of information, entertainment, and communication. ■ If you have more than one computer in your house, or you want to connect more than one television to your cable or satellite TV service, or simply want to play the same music or videos in more than one room, you're a prime prospect for adding data, video, and audio networks to your house.

■ Access to a high-speed information utility is fast becoming an aspect of everyday domestic life; soon it will be as common as telephone, cable TV, and electric wiring are now. This chapter will help you understand not only what a home network has to offer today but how it can prepare your home for tomorrow's technology as it becomes available.

imagining the possibilities

Sharing an Internet connection, computer files, and printers, and expanding your access to music and video services are just a few of the good reasons to include networks in the plans for any new house under construction, or to add them to your existing home. If you subscribe to a high-speed Internet service via DSL or cable modem, a home network can extend that connection to every room in the house. Streaming radio and music services, and music stored on your computer's hard drive, can play through a home network to speakers throughout the house. In the near future, the same network will support so-called smart appliances, controlled remotely via the Internet or your cell phone. It will also support remote monitoring and control devices that you can operate from the computers in your kitchen, bedroom, or home office.

Just as the existing electric wires inside your walls provide power throughout the house, a home's data network can create an electronic central nervous system that supplies information wherever and whenever you need it. And when it's time to sell the house, such network wiring can add value and make the house more attractive to potential buyers.

Installing a home network is becoming more straightforward all the time. The cable, connectors, tools, and equipment you need to complete the job are now available at home centers, larger office supply stores, and computer retailers. Your most difficult task by far will be running new lines through walls. The wiring is low voltage, so it is unlikely that you'll need a permit. (If in doubt, check with your local building department.) However, if you're installing a network panel that requires running a 120-volt line, you will need a permit. This book will equip you to run data, video, audio, and telephone cables through your walls, choose the hardware you need to connect everything together, and configure your computers to communicate through the network you create.

Once a home network panel is installed, changing the service to a given room is as simple as plugging in a patch cord. For example, a bedroom being converted for use as a home office can be quickly linked to a high-speed phone/DSL line. (See pages 96–97 for how to install a network panel.)

data networks

Any family with more than one computer can benefit from installing a network. Even a basic system can connect multiple computers to one Internet source and allow family members to send documents or pictures to a printer from any computer in the house.

The same network that carries e-mail and permits Web surfing can also distribute music and video to your various computers, monitor a camera in the baby's room, or allow you and your family to play multiplayer games. Within a few years, the home network may even turn on your lights and control other household systems and services. Every time another device connects to the network, the entire network becomes more useful.

A household data network connects two or more computers, printers, or other devices, using cables or radio links. A computer connected to the network can exchange with other devices on the same network any information that can be converted to digital data. This can include computer files and commands, text and voice messages, music, and video. The same network can connect Internet access points, video cameras, and printers. In other words, a home computer network can distribute information to and from every room in the house.

Most home networks handle two kinds of data: information that originates outside the local network, including Web pages and e-mail that come in through the Internet; and data that moves from one local device to another, such as files, remote-control commands, and signals from remote cameras and other sensors. The same home network can handle both internal and external data.

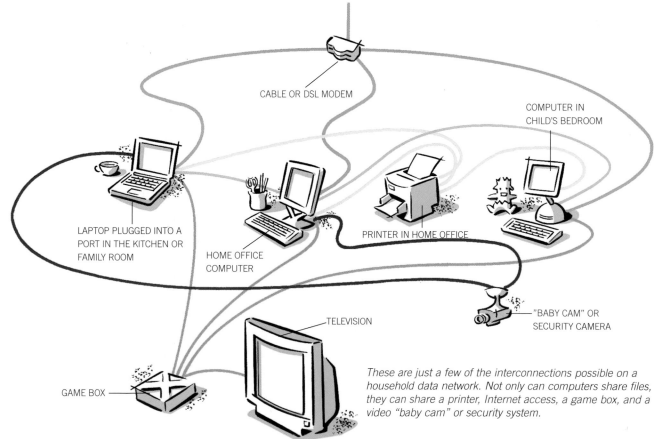

CABLE OR DSL MODEM

COMPUTER IN CHILD'S BEDROOM

LAPTOP PLUGGED INTO A PORT IN THE KITCHEN OR FAMILY ROOM

HOME OFFICE COMPUTER

PRINTER IN HOME OFFICE

TELEVISION

"BABY CAM" OR SECURITY CAMERA

GAME BOX

These are just a few of the interconnections possible on a household data network. Not only can computers share files, they can share a printer, Internet access, a game box, and a video "baby cam" or security system.

Multitaskers who like their choice of a comfortable spot in the house need only plug into a nearby network outlet to send e-mail, check eBay, talk on the phone, or listen to music streaming from the Internet.

INTERNET SERVICE

Many people already turn to the Internet for news reports, music, e-mail, and shopping. They're also becoming increasingly adept at sending photographs and files and participating in live chat services and multiplayer games. The Internet has become a useful tool for everyday living, whether you want to find out how to care for a ficus plant, see if you are still the high bidder for that antique spokeshave, confirm your savings account balance, or check screening times and recent reviews of a new movie.

Until recently, the typical home Internet connection has been a relatively slow data link that places a call to an Internet service provider and connects via a modem (actually a type of converter whose name derives from its MODulator/DEModulator function). Many people, however, are now upgrading to high-speed broadband service. Broadband can connect to your house through a telephone line, cable TV service, or satellite dish. Unlike a modem connection, which requires a new dialup every time you want to use the Internet, broadband service is always on. With broadband, an Internet command can immediately receive a reply from a distant computer.

A network spreads the benefits of the Internet throughout the house. Without a home network, only one computer can connect to the Internet at a time (presuming there's not a separate telephone line for each computer). If other family members want to check for e-mail or read the latest news, they'll have to wait for the connected machine to be free before they can go online. (More likely, they'll start to nag the person using that one computer.) However, a home network can distribute a single Internet connection to two or more computers, so one family member can check for new e-mail while another is researching a homework assignment or swapping messages with friends and a third is listening to a live concert.

Connecting to the Internet through a home network is the best way to get full value from an Internet account— and perhaps the only way to prevent family battles over use of the computer with Internet access.

FILE SHARING

Have you ever wanted to edit a file located on one computer when you're using a second machine? You probably had to make a copy of the file on a floppy disk and carry it to another room. This kind of file transfer is sometimes known as a "sneakernet" connection, because of the walking involved. When all the computers are connected to a network, files located anywhere are accessible from the machine you're currently using. You can use a word processor, a graphics program, or other program to make changes to the file, and you can print the file no matter where it is stored.

Sharing files among your various computers can save a huge amount of time and trouble. You don't have to worry about where you stored a file, or search for the right floppy disk every time you want to work on a project. Just turn on the nearest computer and open the file, no matter where you used it last.

PRINTER SHARING

When you connect a printer to your network, you can print a document from any computer, even if the printer is located in another room. This is especially handy for laptop users who want to plug into a nearby data jack and print a quick copy from the household printer. Just click the Print command, and the computer will automatically send the document through

the network to the printer. If you have more than one printer (maybe a laser printer for black-and-white documents and a color inkjet for pictures and other graphics), you can choose the one best suited for each job.

With a home network, you can plug into any available data port, select a printer anywhere in the house, and print a copy. Gone are the days when you had to save the file to a disk first and carry it to the computer and printer you wanted to use.

MUSIC FILES AND STREAMING AUDIO

A computer linked to the Internet is a great source for audio services. Hundreds of radio stations around the world offer everything from indie rock and bluegrass to live news reports and sports events. Want to listen to jazz from New Orleans, Irish reels from Dublin, or live symphonic concerts from the Berlin Philharmonic? How about play-by-play coverage of your favorite sport, whether it's baseball from Boston or cricket from Bangalore? They're all out there on streaming Internet radio stations that can play through your computer or your stereo system.

It's also possible to store music on a computer's hard drive, or on a specialized device called an audio server, and listen to it through a home network. Whether you download music files through the Internet or copy your own CDs and LPs, your network will allow you to select and play individual music files without the need to handle any physical media. A new generation of audio components can connect your home theater, stereo system, or tabletop boom box directly to a home network. Or, if you prefer, you can use the speakers connected directly to your computer or run an audio cable from the computer to a stereo system.

With a network, the wide world of music is available to your household. Every wired room in the house can access music files and streaming Internet radio stations.

DIGITAL VIDEO

Digital video recorders can use a home network to transfer recorded TV shows, recorded music, and photos from one location to another within the house. For example, if you record your favorite show downstairs, a digital video recorder can send it through the network to the TV in the bedroom. If you have music files stored anywhere on your home network, the recorder can also play that music through any TV set in the house.

A digital video recorder like TiVo records television shows, music, and photos. A network can link it to every television in the house.

MULTIPLAYER GAMES

With a network connection, game players can compete with others in another room through the household network, or anywhere in the world through the Internet. The same network that serves home computers can also connect game consoles, including Sony's PlayStation, Microsoft's Xbox, and Nintendo's GameCube, so players in separate locations can easily participate in the same games.

Many more multiplayer games are available through the Internet. At any time of the day or night, there are thousands of people around the world who are connected to online servers offering everything from chess and backgammon to the latest adventure games. If you're looking for competition, there's almost always somebody out there ready to play.

Too rainy for golf? Arrange a foursome on the Internet and play from the comfort of your study. With a network, any computer in the household has access to multiplayer games.

VIDEO CAMERAS

Do you need to keep an eye on your children in another room or see who's knocking at your front door? Or maybe conduct a "face-to-face" conversation with a family member in another part of the house? Stand-alone network cameras can transmit sound and pictures from remote locations to any computer connected to your home network or to the Internet. You can keep an image from a remote camera open in a separate window on the computer's screen while you do other work, or switch to the camera's output when you want to see what's happening in that room.

A networked video camera can become a "baby cam" that lets you view your child's room from elsewhere in the house.

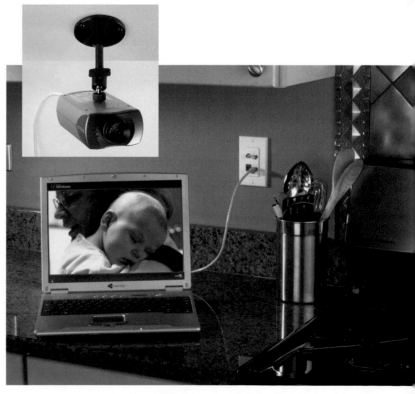

coming attractions

Our great-grandparents installed wires in their homes in order to replace gas lamps with electric lights. They never imagined that the same wiring would provide power to today's air conditioners, microwave ovens, electric toothbrushes, home theater systems, and computers. It's the same with network wiring: Within the next few years, we could be using home networks for purposes not yet even imagined.

One possibility is that the next generation of appliances, home entertainment systems, and maybe even water heaters and furnaces will have network ports for remote access and control through a home network. But what about a remote alarm that warns you when the garage door has been left open or the back door left unlocked? And how long will it be before the well-equipped kitchen has a compact control panel that monitors the temperature in every room of the house and provides controls for all of the household systems? Manufacturers have already developed ovens (right) that can be cued remotely via a cell phone or the Internet to thaw and cook dinner.

Some prognosticators await the advent of the "smart" refrigerator. This networked fridge would monitor the temperature in the freezer section and automatically send an alarm signal or an e-mail message if the temperature rises above a preset level and the ice cream starts to melt. It could even keep track of the "best before" dates on the milk and the cottage cheese, or create a weekly shopping list that automatically tells you when it's time to buy more eggs or orange juice.

A quick chat with your oven may be all it takes to change your cooking plans. Smart appliances have been developed that will allow you to put a dish in the oven before going to bed and program the appliance to refrigerate and then cook the dish by dinnertime the next day. The appliance can send a text message asking, "Do you still want me to have this dish ready by 7:00 p.m.?" If your plans change, you can instruct the appliance accordingly—even from your cell phone.

Soon, major appliances may be equipped to run their own periodic diagnostic tests and—by means of a network system—actually call for repair services as they are needed.

The likelihood that these and other such gadgets will be the norm in the not so distant future underlines the practicality of a versatile and expandable home network.

telephones, video, and audio

While you're planning and installing a home data network, you should also consider your requirements for other kinds of information wiring, including telephones, video, and audio. As long as you're cutting holes in the walls for your computer network, consider adding or expanding other information services at the same time—the same cable runs, wall plates, and distribution centers can serve all four types of wiring. The additional cost of the extra wire is small, and it will more than pay for itself when you discover that you really do need that unexpected extension telephone or an additional cable TV connection. If the wires and outlets are already in place, then setting up a new phone, television, or computer will be a simple 5-minute job instead of a major project that can take all day.

TELEPHONE WIRING

Telephones aren't the only devices that connect to household telephone wiring. Base stations for cordless phones, answering machines, fax

machines, modems, set-top cable TV boxes, and security systems all use the public telephone network to communicate with the outside world. You may have extension phones in your kitchen, bedrooms, and other locations already, but in today's wired world, most homeowners find it helpful to have at least one or two telephone outlets in just about every room.

It's not uncommon for a household to have two or more separate telephone lines. In addition to the main line that the family uses for voice calls, there may be a second line for teens and preteens to use for voice and modem calls. Many homes also have a fax line and a line for the security alarm. And if you have a home-based business, or if you telecommute or often bring work home from the office, it's not unusual to install yet another dedicated voice line for business use.

DirecTV, Dish Network, and TiVo all use telephone lines to communicate with their set-top boxes. They might not need a full-time phone line, but they do need access to an outlet.

A network gives you the versatility to plug in your phones and other equipment exactly where you want them. Will you need another line when

The base station for a cordless telephone is just one of the many pieces of hardware tied into your home's telephone system. A home network lends order to a welter of connections. Answering machines, fax machines, pay-per-view setups, and security systems all connect to old-fashioned phone lines.

your children get older? Do you need a separate fax number for your home office? Do you plan to install an alarm system that will need a dedicated line to communicate with the monitoring center? A well-planned network provides a phone line to every room in the house where a phone might be used, and perhaps more than one line in the kitchen or the home office.

As your family grows older and your life changes, your telephone requirements will likely change too. So it's a good idea to have a flexible telephone system that will let you add, move, and change your telephone connections. Once wires have been run from every telephone outlet back to a central network panel, it's a simple matter to add new phones and related devices to make the most efficient use of the various telephone lines coming into the house.

VIDEO PROGRAMMING

Whether video programming comes into the house through a cable TV subscription, a satellite dish, or an old-fashioned rooftop antenna, it is handy to have a way to distribute those signals to several rooms. Within your home, the same video cables that bring in programs and data from the outside can also distribute movies and other programs from a VCR or a DVD player.

TV sets and home theater systems in the family room, the kitchen, and every bedroom all need access to video signals. If you use a cable modem to connect to the Internet, you'll need an outlet next to one of your computers. Most cable and satellite TV services also offer audio programs from broadcast FM radio stations, their own music

Drawing upon the signal from a satellite dish, cable, or even a rooftop antenna, your home network can forward programming to any room in the house.

Adding a video component to your home network will enhance the clarity and flexibility of entertainment programming. It will also allow you to distribute throughout the house music and radio programs available from cable and satellite sources.

services, or both, so you may want to consider a cable outlet in every room that has a radio, including the bathrooms, garage, and basement.

AUDIO NETWORKS

Ever find yourself tuning several radios to the same station so you can listen to your favorite programs while doing household chores? Your stereo can play compact discs, FM radio, computer files, tapes, and maybe even a turntable for your old LPs, providing high-fidelity music in one or two rooms. But you're out of luck if you leave that immediate vicinity unless you extend the reach of your sound system with an audio network. With speakers connected to a common program source, you can listen to the same music or spoken-word programming as you travel from room to room. Whether the speakers are set into the walls or ceiling or simply rest on shelves or the floor, a

household audio system can distribute the sounds to whatever rooms you choose. If you and your family don't share the same tastes in music, you can even direct different programs to different locations.

Whole-house audio wiring isn't as common (or as essential) as data, telephone, and video networking, but it's easy enough to include when you're stringing those other cables. It's a nice feature to consider, especially if you and your family are serious music lovers.

If you're on the fringes of the signal range from a distant or low-power FM station that features your favorite kind of music, you may want to add an external antenna, even if you get your TV service from cable or satellite. By linking the antenna to an FM receiver that is in turn hooked up to the network, the entire household can enjoy the improved reception.

planning your home network

THE FIRST STEP IN INSTALLING A HOME NETWORK is to create a detailed plan. Your plan should identify the services that the network will provide, the location of each network access point, and the routes that the cables will follow from the service entry through the control center to each outlet. It's a lot easier to change locations and add services during the planning stage, before you start cutting through the walls and floors. The ideal home network wiring plan will also build in avenues for pulling new lines and adding new features in the future. This chapter will help you plan each aspect of your home network. It also examines the role of wireless technology in a network (see page 23). ■ Start by drawing up a floor plan for each story of the house, including the attic and basement. Closets are often useful for hiding cable runs; include them in your plan. In each room, make a list of the devices that will connect to your network: computers, printers, telephones, TVs, remote speakers, and so forth. Each device needs a wall outlet, as close to the device as possible. Include locations for new devices that may be added later. The floor plan should also identify where the telephone lines and cable TV or satellite dish cables enter the house.

building in flexibility

Most home networks include outlets in the living room, the bedrooms, the kitchen, the home office, and every other room that might have a telephone, a computer, a television, or a home entertainment system. Don't forget bathrooms; it's easy to install a telephone and speakers for music from CDs or streaming Internet audio.

The most flexible approach is to install what is called a structured wiring bundle from the network panel to each outlet plate. Such a bundle includes three data cables (which can also be used for telephones) and one or two coaxial cables for video. Remember that a network installed today will remain in place for many years, so it's important to make updates and changes as easy to accommodate as possible. It's generally best not to settle for installing data and video outlets only in the locations where computers and TV sets are

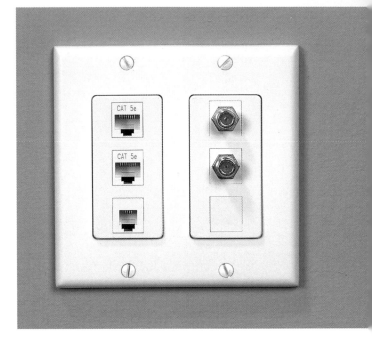

This outlet includes two data jacks (each of which can act as anything from a high-speed line to a standard telephone line), a phone jack, and two video jacks—as well as a blank port for future needs. It is the termination point for a bundle of three CAT 5e and two coaxial cables.

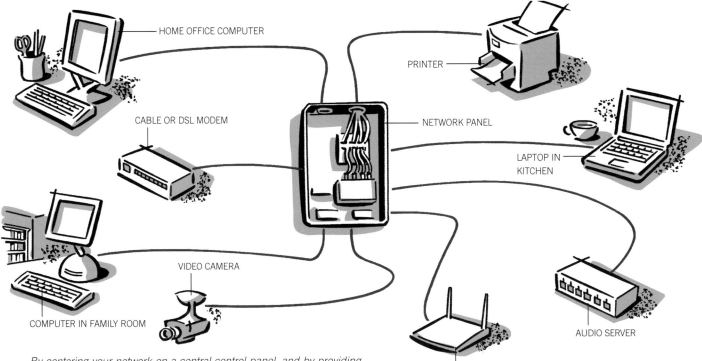

HOME OFFICE COMPUTER

PRINTER

CABLE OR DSL MODEM

NETWORK PANEL

LAPTOP IN KITCHEN

COMPUTER IN FAMILY ROOM

VIDEO CAMERA

WIRELESS ACCESS POINT

AUDIO SERVER

By centering your network on a central control panel, and by providing rooms with a combination of cables (as reflected in the outlet above right), you can easily change the services provided to each room.

located today. By the time your toddler reaches his teens, it's inevitable that he will want a computer with an Internet link in his bedroom. When your teenage daughter moves away to college, her room may turn into a home office. Well-designed home network wiring will support these changes (and others that you don't expect) with just a few adjustments at the network panel (see photo page 6).

Next, choose a spot for the network panel. Look for a central location so as to minimize long cable runs. And it should be in an area of the house where the temperature is stable. A closet, upstairs laundry area, or utility room is ideal. Avoid attics and garages. Do not place your control panel next to breaker panels or subpanels.

Once the network is up and running, the only time it will be necessary to open the panel is when you want to add, move, or change a network service. Thus it doesn't need to be at the center of daily household activity, but it should be relatively easy for you to reach without climbing a ladder or crawling through a tangle of bicycles, storage boxes, and miscellaneous junk.

A schematic drawing of a household network should resemble a big star, or the spokes of an old wagon wheel, with the control panel at the center. This is often called a "home run" network, because all the cables run to the central panel. Unlike the electric wiring of your home, in which many outlets can share a single cable back to the fuse box or the circuit breaker panel, the wiring for your network should have separate

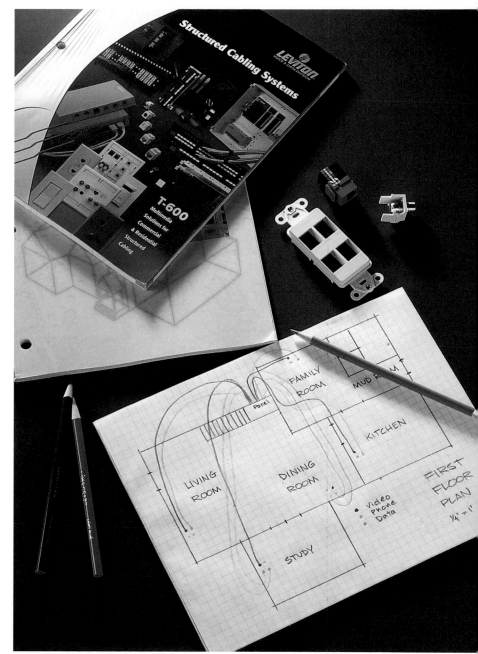

On your floor plan, indicate the new lines that will run from each outlet to the network panel. Use different colors to indicate whether the line is voice/data, coaxial, or audio.

cables from each outlet running directly to the network panel.

Think through the possible routes that the cables can follow from each outlet to the central network panel. Whenever possible, try to run the cables up from the crawl space or basement, or and simplify future alterations to the network by providing an easy route for fishing cables, without cutting additional holes. (If possible, plan to locate your network panel near this pipe.)

PLANNING YOUR DATA NETWORK

A household data network includes several elements: computers; a router that links to the Internet; additional devices such as a printer, a video camera, or an audio server; and a hub (sometimes combined in the router) that connects everything. As discussed in the preceding chapter, it is likely that, within the next few years, still more devices will use the same network to receive commands and transmit information—possibly kitchen appliances and the systems that control lights, heating, and air conditioning. Therefore, the wiring that supports a data network should extend to just about every room of the house.

On the other hand, it's not absolutely necessary to wire the entire house just to share a printer and connect multiple computers to the Internet. A simpler network, with all the cables connected to a hub next to one of the computers, will serve perfectly well. It's a decision about whether to invest in the system now, before you actually need the capacity, or later, when it's time to expand.

Today's data networks are like electric wiring a hundred years ago. Many old houses have just one or two AC outlets in each room, which isn't enough to meet today's demand. A house with network service in only a few locations might be adequate today, but tomorrow's wired home will almost certainly require more data access points. Planning and installing the network with expansion in mind will cost a little more time and money now, but when you need additional service down the road, you'll be able to add it with a lot less trouble.

In the back of a closet or some other out-of-sight location, install a 2-inch PVC plumbing pipe between the crawl space or basement and the attic. Use it as a convenient channel for pulling cable—now and in the future.

down from the attic to the location of an outlet. If the house has more than one floor, look for an out-of-sight place where you can run a 1½-inch or 2-inch PVC pipe from the crawl space or basement to the attic. Inside a wall, inside a closet, and next to a plumbing stack are all workable options. This pipe will serve your immediate needs

A DATA NETWORK

COMPUTER IN CHILD'S BEDROOM

HOME OFFICE COMPUTER

TELEVISION

GAME BOX

NETWORK PANEL

LAPTOP IN KITCHEN

SECURITY CAMERA

Here is one example of how computers and related devices might be linked through a centrally located network panel. Note that a game box and a security video camera can be included in the system.

LOCATING NETWORK OUTLETS

At a minimum, your data network should have access points near every computer, including in the home office, den or study, and each bedroom. If there are video game enthusiasts in the family, or if you use a personal video recorder (PVR), it's a good idea to install a dual outlet for both data and video near each television set and game console. In the kitchen, place an outlet on the wall near a counter for computer and television connections. And if you are wiring with an eye toward the future, install outlets with two data connections out of sight close to the refrigerator and other appliances (see page 12).

For a fully networked house, the rule of thumb is to install at least two data outlets, plus a video cable outlet and a telephone outlet and possibly an audio outlet, in every major room. All the cables from these outlets should run through the walls directly to the central network panel. These outlets can share a single flush-mounted wall plate or surface-mounted box, or they can be located on separate walls, close to the devices that will be connected to them. On the other hand, it's entirely possible to get carried away with installing more cables than you really need. If your immediate goal is simply to connect all your household computers to the Internet, a single outlet near each computer might be all you need.

If possible, avoid placing network outlets on outside walls that are filled with insulating material. It's a lot easier to fish a cable through the empty space of an interior wall than to fight with a lot of foam or spun fiber.

FACEPLATE

JACK PLATE

CAP

DATA JACK

CAT 5e — DATA JACK

This multifunction outlet includes two pairs of speaker wire connectors, two phone or data ports, and two video ports—a workable setup for a home entertainment center.

A basic combination for an outlet in a bedroom might include one video port, and two data/phone ports, each of which accepts an eight-wire (high-speed type) plug (see page 55) used for data, or the type of four-wire plug found on most phones.

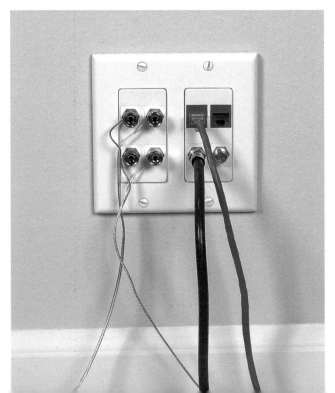

WIRED OR WIRELESS?

A wireless network that uses radio signals can be an attractive alternative to a wired household network. Networks that follow the so-called Wi-Fi wireless standards use one or more radio access points to cover the entire house and the surrounding area, including outdoor decks, the backyard, and nearby buildings, such as a detached garage.

A Wi-Fi network might be the best choice when it's not practical or possible to drill holes for network cables. For example, a wireless network is the only way to go if you want to carry a single computer from room to room, or use a laptop or other portable computer from a picnic table or hammock in the backyard. And the same Wi-Fi interface card you use at home can also connect a laptop computer to public Wi-Fi "hot spots" in coffee shops, airports, schools, and libraries.

However, a Wi-Fi network has several disadvantages compared with a wired network. First, Wi-Fi uses radio signals, which are not as secure as network wiring. A dedicated intruder can monitor Wi-Fi signals and steal data, including e-mail passwords, credit card numbers, and private messages. It's possible to use encryption and other methods to reduce the danger of data theft, but such methods are less than perfect.

Second, Wi-Fi signals don't stop at the property line. So the same wireless network that supplies service to your house will also allow neighbors and "drive-by" networkers to use your system from up to 300 feet away without your permission. If your neighbors have their own Wi-Fi networks, you'll have to configure both systems to reduce potential interference.

Third, Wi-Fi networks share an unlicensed portion of the radio spectrum with a variety of other

This wireless hub is one of many available from electronic stores, computer outlets, and catalogs. To use a hub, you'll need a wireless network adapter inside your computer or connected through the USB port.

services, including some microwave ovens and cordless telephones. The radio signals from these other devices can reduce the quality of a wireless data network. In addition, Wi-Fi signals can interfere with some cordless phones.

And finally, the data-handling capacity of a Wi-Fi network is lower than that of a wired network. This may not make much difference when computers on the network are exchanging files or using the Internet, but it can be a problem for people who want to play multiuser games or watch movies online.

So a wireless network is a trade-off between convenience and security. Wireless might be easier to install, but a wired network will almost always be faster, safer, and more flexible.

The ideal home network might be a combination of both wired and wireless links. Use wires to connect computers, printers, and other network devices in the family room, home office, kitchen, bedrooms, and other permanent locations, and add a wireless access point for portable computers and outdoor use. To reduce the danger of data theft and unauthorized access, turn off the wireless access point when it's not in use.

Even if you currently use a very basic modem, by installing a data line you are prepared for an upgrade to higher-speed service.

DSL service uses standard phone lines to achieve high-speed Internet service. To do this, a DSL modem (above) must be attached to your incoming phone line. Underground cables often terminate in a box attached to the house (below).

ADDING HIGH-SPEED INTERNET SERVICE

Sharing an Internet connection is one of the main reasons to install a home network. Access to the Internet can take any one of these forms:

- A dial-out telephone line is the least costly way to connect to the Internet, but it's also the slowest. To connect to the Internet, the computer places a telephone call to a service provider, using a modem—either a separate unit (shown at left) or an internal modem built into your computer. The maximum data transfer speed is 53 kilobits per second (Kbps), though in reality it typically runs at 36–48 Kbps.

- DSL (Digital Subscriber Link) service connects to the Internet through telephone lines, but it doesn't interfere with traditional "dial tone" service, so it's possible to place and receive telephone calls while you're using the Internet. In most locations, DSL service is available only within about three miles of a telephone central office (CO) where the Internet access lines and switching equipment are housed.

- Cable modem service uses the same connection that provides cable TV service. The cable company might advertise data speeds "up to 3.5 Mbps (megabits per second)" but that "up to" can be misleading, because the actual speed depends on the number of neighbors who share a cable. In practice, an inbound cable modem connection (from the Internet to your computer) is likely to operate at about the same speed as a DSL line. Outbound speed (from your computer to the Internet) is slower, typically about 128 to 256 Kbps.

- Satellite Internet service uses a rooftop dish antenna to send and receive data. Satellite service is more expensive than cable or DSL, but it's often the only way to obtain a relatively high-speed connection outside of a metropolitan area. The maximum download (inbound) speed is about 500 Kbps, but that can drop to as little as

150 Kbps during peak demand times. Upload (outbound) speed is about 80 Kbps.

Cable, DSL, and satellite connections are often described as "broadband" service because they all provide access to the Internet at high speed. In practice, the cost and performance of cable and DSL connections are about the same, especially if both services are available and the service providers are competing for business. If both are available, look for the best combination of price and performance. Satellite is almost always a last option; both cable and DSL offer superior service at a lower price. If neither is available, however, satellite is still an improvement over a dial-up connection.

All major types of broadband Internet service—DSL, cable, satellite, and point-to-multipoint wireless—connect to a home network the same way. Each service needs a gateway device that provides a signal to the local network's hub. All the other devices that are connected to the same hub can exchange data with the Internet through the shared connection.

By contrast, Internet access through a modem and a telephone line connects directly to a single computer. To extend the connection to other computers on the same network, both Microsoft Windows and Apple's Macintosh operating systems include Internet connection sharing features.

Your home can connect to the Internet by means of a satellite dish, through a phone line (with or without DSL enhancement), or via your television cable service. Incoming lines are typically overhead for older homes, underground for newer ones.

DSL VIA PHONE LINE

INTERNET ACCESS VIA SATELLITE DISH

CABLE MODEM SERVICE

NETWORKING VIDEO CAMERAS

Network cameras combine the functions of a video camera and a network server in a single compact unit that connects directly to a data network. Any computer connected to the network can display the image from the camera—and with some models relay the sounds from a built-in microphone—through a Web browser such as Microsoft Internet Explorer or Netscape Navigator. Some network cameras can also be configured to transmit images to the Internet so that they're accessible anywhere in the world. A camera can connect to your home network through either a data cable or a Wi-Fi wireless link.

As discussed in the earlier chapter, a network camera can be a great way to keep track of activity in another part of the house, such as a nursery or a front door. And as with most other technology, the price of network cameras is likely to drop as they become more common over the next several years. So if you anticipate particular safety or security needs in your household, it may be a good idea to include several locations for cameras in your network plan. If a data outlet is already available, installing a new camera is just a matter of plugging in a cable and setting a few options.

While a video camera for monitoring your sleeping child might be your only immediate need, consider wiring your home for the future. The backyard play area, driveway, and front entryway are other locations worth considering.

SELECTING A ROUTER AND HUB

Every data network needs a router (shown below) to link up to the outside world via the Internet. The router also performs the housekeeping tasks that are necessary to keep a network running. It assigns a separate local address to each device on the network and converts those addresses to and from the single address that identifies the local network to the rest of the world. Many routers designed specifically for home networks and small businesses also include built-in firewall software that turns away any unauthorized attempt to gain access to the computers on the network.

The best choice for a home network is usually a router that includes a gateway to and from a broadband Internet connection, and one that supports both 10baseT (10 Mbps) and 100baseT (100 Mbps) connections. These devices are widely available from computer retailers and office supply stores. Look for a router labeled specially for small office and home office (SOHO) networks rather than the more expensive versions intended for commercial data centers. Since the router is the interface between the home network and the Internet, it should be located close to the access point for the service providing your Internet access. For DSL connections, that's a telephone outlet; for cable or satellite, use a video (cable TV) outlet. The Internet service provider will specify or supply a modem unit that will convert the signals to and from the TV cable, telephone line, or satellite dish to a format that the network hub can handle.

The router is connected to (and sometimes built into) a hub (or an interchangeable and increasingly popular device known as a switch).

When shopping for a hub, look for SOHO types (small office, home office) rather than those designed for commercial use. A peripheral unit (above) is the simplest approach; a network panel can include a built-in hub (below).

As the name suggests, the hub is at the center of the network. Every computer, printer, video camera, audio server, or other device on the network requires a separate connection to the hub, called a port. A central hub is the go-between that lets computers talk to each other and, through a router, to the Internet. It also transfers commands and data between the local network and the Internet. When a computer requests a file from a second computer or sends a command to check

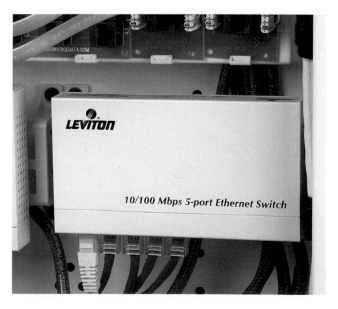

for new e-mail through the Internet, it sends an instruction to the hub, which in turn passes it along to the destination. When the target for this request responds, it sends an answer back to the originator through the same network hub.

Either a cable or a wireless link connects each network device to the hub. Network hubs come in several sizes, generally with 4 to 12 ports but sometimes more. It's also possible to expand a network by connecting two or more hubs together.

Flashing lights on the face of the hub light and go dark to indicate network activity on each port. If the network includes a central control panel, that's a logical location for the hub, but it might not be the best place if it's combined with a router. During installation, and when you are talking with the Internet service provider's customer support center by telephone, it can be very helpful to watch the lights on the router and the modem as a technician sends test signals to your computer. So placing the router next to a computer might be a better choice than an out-of-the-way network panel. You can then connect it to one or more additional hubs at the control center, as shown in the diagram below.

One other type of hub is worth considering for a home network. Several manufacturers offer hybrid units that combine the functions of a wired multiport network switch and a wireless access point, so that some computers and other devices can connect through data cables and others via Wi-Fi links. If your network will include both wired and wireless hubs, a hybrid hub could be the best choice.

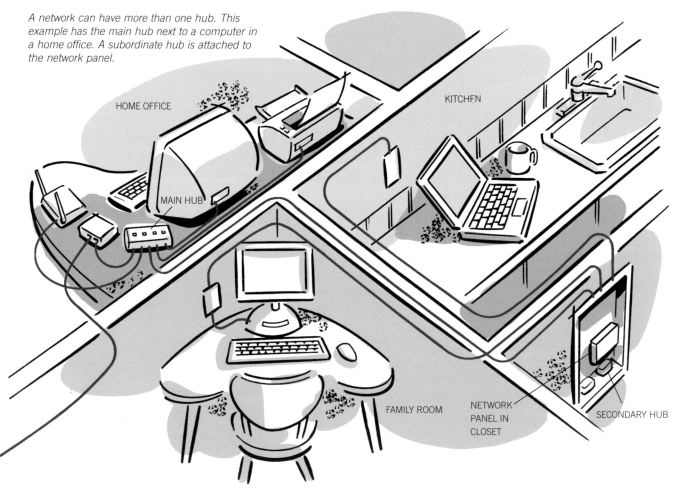

A network can have more than one hub. This example has the main hub next to a computer in a home office. A subordinate hub is attached to the network panel.

HOME OFFICE

MAIN HUB

KITCHEN

FAMILY ROOM

NETWORK PANEL IN CLOSET

SECONDARY HUB

planning a video network

Information from a cable TV service, a satellite dish, or a rooftop antenna travels through coaxial cable (below). Coaxial cable uses connectors that are different from the twisted pairs and multipin plugs used in data and telephone networks. However, these cables can run side by side and use the same outlet plates.

How many video outlets to install is a decision you'll need to make based on how much you use video currently and what you anticipate your future needs to be. However, you'll be more than covered if you have at least one multipurpose outlet (disassembled, at right) in each room. These provide all three types of signal—computer data, video, and telephone—with speaker connectors thrown in as well. The alternative is to provide only the wiring and outlets that are necessary to support the equipment currently at each location: video to the TV sets, data to the computers, and telephone to the phones. The multipurpose outlet approach is almost always a better choice; over time, the specific requirements in each room will probably change.

Within the next few years, video-on-demand services will offer movies, sports events, and other programs through the Internet, so a data outlet near every TV along with the video connector is a particularly good idea.

Of course, a household video network can be as simple as a connection to the cable or satellite TV service at every set. But with a little more effort and equipment, the same cables can also share movies and other programs from a single VCR or DVD player among all the televisions in

Standard coaxial cable (shown with black or white sheathing) is fine for home use, though some people spring for studio-grade cable (blue).

the house. They can also distribute FM radio programs and add signals from a rooftop antenna that may not be available through the cable or satellite service. So it's not out of the question to install at least one video outlet in every room of the house, including the kitchen and bathrooms.

In some locations a single outlet might not be enough. Most amplifiers that boost an incoming video signal operate in only one direction, so any device that transmits video or data to the system should use a cable that bypasses the amplifier. For example, the signal from a VCR or DVD should travel to the network panel on a separate cable from the one that distributes video signals to the TV set in the same room. And if the broadband Internet access uses a cable modem, the modem should connect to the network panel through a dedicated cable.

VIDEO JACK

FACEPLATE

FACEPLATE INSERT

AUDIO JACK

DATA JACK

TV ON A COMPUTER MONITOR

Even if there's not a TV set in every room, it's often a good idea to include a video outlet along with just about every data outlet. In locations where space is limited, a computer can double as a TV set. With either an expansion card inside the computer or a module that connects to the computer's external USB port, the computer can display television programs on its monitor and play the audio through its speakers.

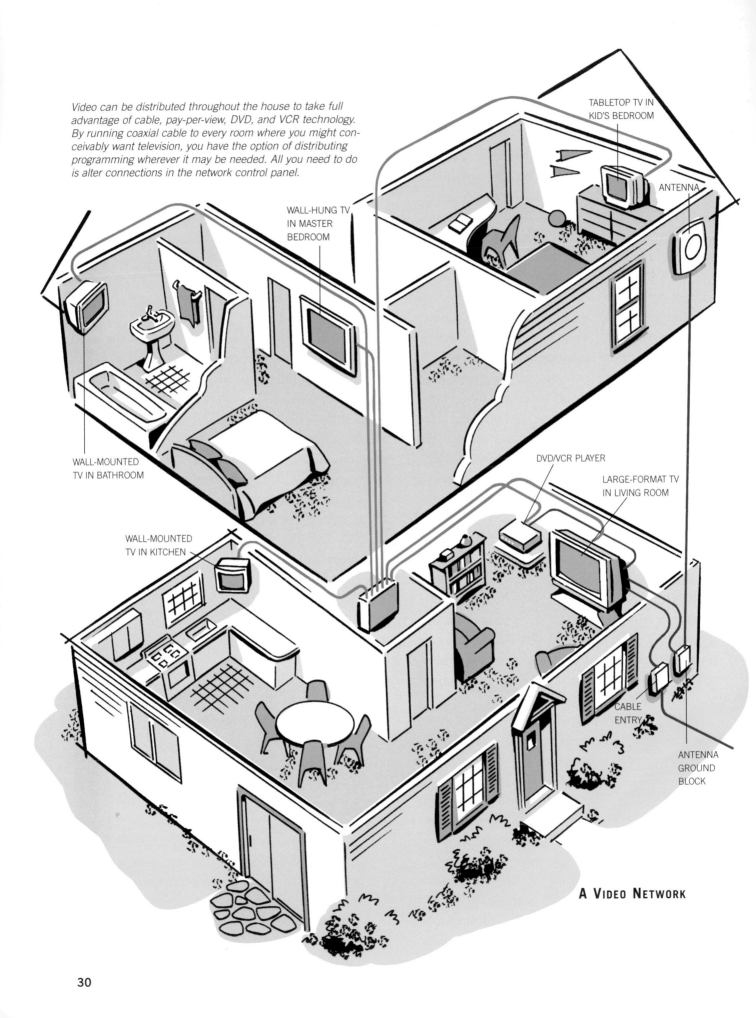

Video can be distributed throughout the house to take full advantage of cable, pay-per-view, DVD, and VCR technology. By running coaxial cable to every room where you might conceivably want television, you have the option of distributing programming wherever it may be needed. All you need to do is alter connections in the network control panel.

TABLETOP TV IN KID'S BEDROOM

ANTENNA

WALL-HUNG TV IN MASTER BEDROOM

WALL-MOUNTED TV IN BATHROOM

DVD/VCR PLAYER

LARGE-FORMAT TV IN LIVING ROOM

WALL-MOUNTED TV IN KITCHEN

CABLE ENTRY

ANTENNA GROUND BLOCK

A VIDEO NETWORK

A home entertainment system is a primary destination for incoming video lines carrying cable or satellite service. It is also a source of DVD or VCR programming, which can be routed elsewhere in the house.

ADDING LOCAL SOURCES

A basic video distribution system takes incoming signals from a cable TV service, a satellite dish, or a roof antenna and sends them to television sets (or computer monitors; see box, page 29) and FM radios throughout the house. A more complex system can add to the package of program channels supplied via cable or satellite; signals from local sources, including movies from a VCR or DVD player; images from a video camera; or broadcast programming from a rooftop antenna.

Every room that contains a program source, such as a VCR or DVD player, should have two video cables to the central network panel. One can carry signals from the source device to the network panel; the other can carry programs from all sources to the TV set and other destination devices. At the network control panel, modulators and signal combiners will add the local channels to the video stream and assign them to otherwise unused channels.

The video network plan should include a list of sources and a list of destinations. Sources might include the service entry for cable TV, the satellite receiver, or the cable from the roof antenna. Also list devices that originate TV signals, such as a

DVD player or VCR. If the cable TV service also provides Internet access through a cable modem, the modem is also a source. Destinations include every TV set and FM radio and the cable modem. Set-top boxes that decode cable signals and PVR (personal video recorder) systems such as TiVo usually connect between the wall outlet and the set, so they aren't separate destinations.

Begin planning the video component of your network with a listing of video sources (such as cable, satellite, and DVD or VCR player), and the destinations to which you want to connect their service.

planning the telephone network

A plan for the telephone component of your household network should specify first the number of telephone lines coming into the house. It should also identify the location of each extension telephone and all the devices that use each line. These devices may include fax machines, answering machines, computers with modems, and alarm systems. For the greatest possible flexibility, each instrument should plug into a separate wall outlet, although it's easy to add more outlets if two or more devices in a room share the same phone line. You can buy a wall plate that holds up to eight separate data, video, and telephone outlets.

The outlet for a tabletop telephone can be anywhere within reach of a cord, but a wall phone must have a special connector and mounting plate (see page 53) at the exact location where the phone will hang on the wall. Wall phones are very common in kitchens, but they can also be handy in shops, studios, laundry rooms—even bathrooms. Your plan should specifically identify each wall phone and its location.

In a residential system, each telephone line usually requires two wires, called tip and ring, to connect each telephone set to the central office. There are exceptions, but a POTS (plain old telephone service) line is a two-wire system. Standard

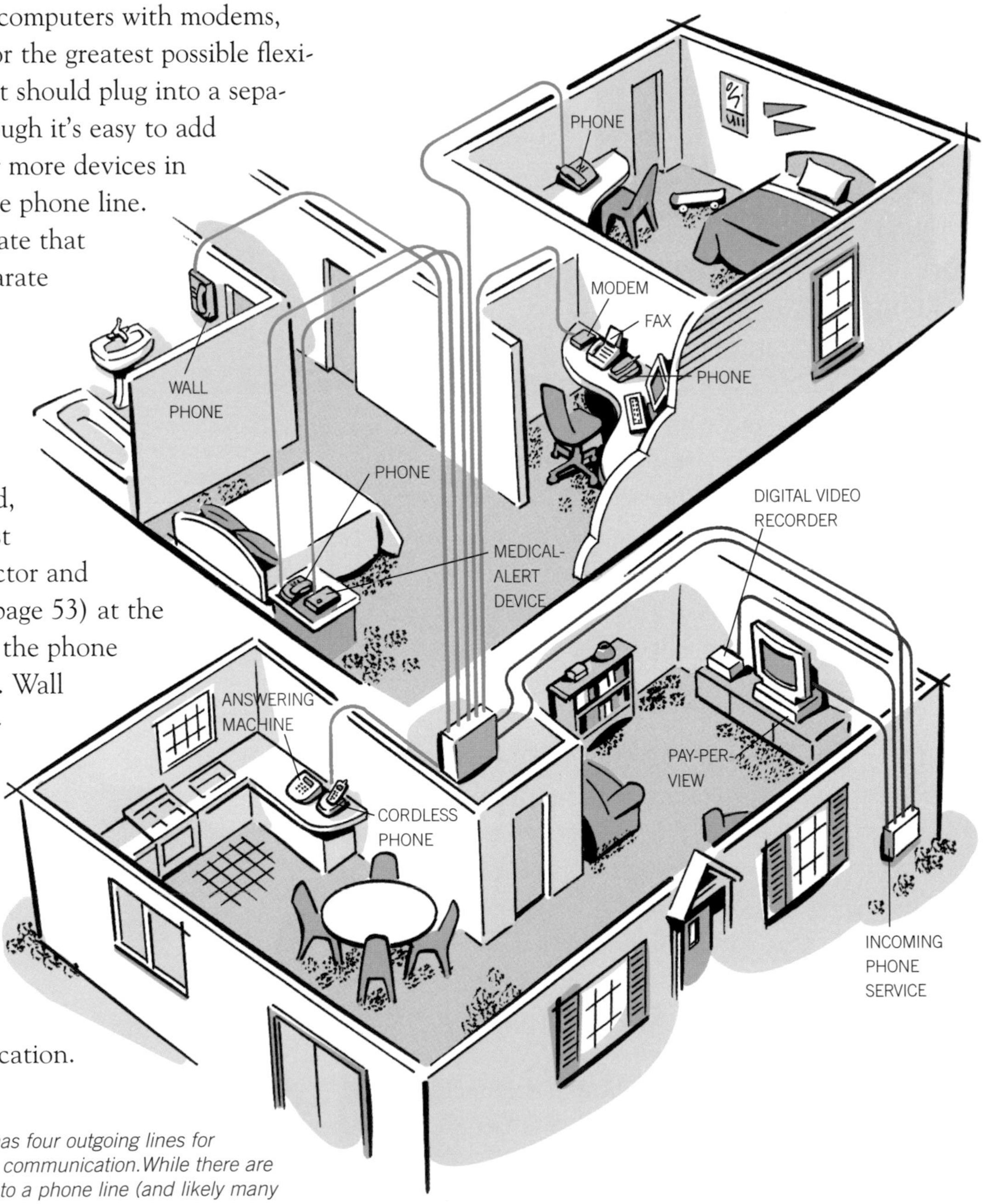

PHONE

MODEM

FAX

PHONE

WALL PHONE

PHONE

DIGITAL VIDEO RECORDER

MEDICAL-ALERT DEVICE

PAY-PER-VIEW

ANSWERING MACHINE

CORDLESS PHONE

INCOMING PHONE SERVICE

The home illustrated here has four outgoing lines for household and home office communication. While there are many devices that connect to a phone line (and likely many more to come), these are some of the more common ones.

telephone cables have four wires, and the CAT 5e data cables used for computer networks have eight wires, so it's common to carry two or more phone lines in a single cable and split them at the wall outlet.

If you're wiring your network for the future, it's best to include at least one telephone outlet in each wall plate, along with the data and video outlets. If it becomes necessary to add a second outlet later, it's easy enough to connect it to the existing wiring.

Just about every existing house already has some inside telephone wiring and outlets in place. It's okay to continue using those outlets if they're in convenient locations, but they won't be tied into the network you're creating and thus won't provide much flexibility. In the long run it's better to connect each incoming telephone line to the network panel and to tie all of your telephone outlets into the network. Even if you don't use all of the new phone outlets now, they'll be ready when you need them.

CORDLESS PHONES

Cordless phones are extremely convenient because they make it easy to carry the handset from room to room. However, even if the portable handset itself doesn't have a wire connecting it to the wall, it requires a base station that exchanges radio signals with the cordless handset and passes them to and from the wired telephone system. The same base station also recharges the battery in the handset when it's resting in the cradle.

The best location for a cordless phone base station is either a spot that's close to the center of the house or else somewhere in the room where the phone will be answered most often.

A telephone network can use standard telephone cable (top) with four wires, but CAT 5e cable (sold in various colors), with eight wires, gives you latitude for voice or high-speed data transmission.

A cordless phone (below), not to be mistaken for a cell phone, has a base station that requires a standard 120-volt receptacle and a phone outlet.

AVOIDING INTERFERENCE ON CORDLESS PHONES

Remember that some cordless phones use the same radio frequencies as Wi-Fi data networks. The two services can interfere with each other, which can add noise to the telephone line and slow down the data connection. So it's best to look for a phone that uses a different frequency range if you have a Wi-Fi network.

If your Wi-Fi network uses this standard:	Avoid cordless phones using this frequency:
802.11b	2.4 GHz
802.11g	2.4 GHz
802.11a	5.8 GHz

OTHER DEVICES ON A PHONE LINE

In addition to telephones, there are a number of devices that use the public telephone network to communicate. Medical monitoring equipment, alarm systems, and some set-top boxes used with cable TV services are all equipped to automatically "phone home" when they need to send a command or transmit data to a monitoring service.

Some devices, including answering machines, modems, and fax machines, have a built-in pass-through outlet, so they don't need additional wall outlets. But other devices may require their own connections. If possible, try to include enough telephone outlets in your network plan to provide access for additional telephone-related boxes that you may need later.

THE SERVICE ENTRY

The service entry is the point where the telephone cables from the pole or under the ground enter your house. It's usually a box mounted on the side of the house, but in older homes the cable from the pole passes through the wall to a service entry in the basement or a utility room. There's usually a short wire from the service entry to a terminal block or terminal strip inside the house, where all the extension phones connect to the telephone line. Often, it is easiest to find the box on the outside of the house, then look for the strip indoors.

When more than one telephone line comes into the house, a single service entry and terminal block might support multiple lines. Each line is

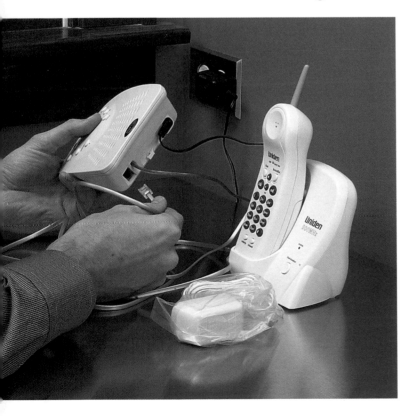

This answering machine includes a pass-through outlet into which another device, like this cordless phone base, can be plugged. Telephone service runs to the answering machine, then on to the cordless phone.

electrically isolated, but they all might terminate in the same place.

In a structured wiring system, each pair of telephone wires (there are two pairs in the typical phone cable) connects one line from the terminal block or service entry to the network control panel. Cables from the outlets throughout the house also terminate at the control panel. A distribution module in the network panel connects each incoming telephone line to one or more outlets. To change the line connected to an outlet, you need only move a patch cord on the network panel.

Telephone lines are not for telephones alone. Devices such as modems, answering machines, and fax machines are just a few that must connect to a phone line to do their jobs.

MODEM

FAX MACHINE

ANSWERING MACHINE

A service entry panel like this one for overhead telephone lines generally marks the point at which the phone company's responsibility ends and yours begins.

Many newer homes have underground phone lines, terminating at a service entry panel like the one below.

TELEPHONE NETWORK INTERFACE

TELEPHONE NETWORK INTERFACE

planning an audio network

A household audio network distributes sounds from a central CD player, radio, or other source to additional speakers elsewhere in the house. Combined with a digital audio server or a computer, an audio network can also play music stored on a hard drive and programs from out-of-town radio stations, delivered via the Internet. Home audio networks can be relatively simple systems that play the same music in every room, or more complex arrangements that direct different programs to different locations within the house. A home network doesn't always include audio distribution, but it's often a good idea to plan audio wiring at the same time as data, telephone, and video wiring.

It's important to understand how an audio system works before you start planning a household audio distribution system, because the design of the system will determine the location of equipment and the type of wiring that carries the audio programs. Specifically, any sound system includes three elements: one or more program sources that convert stored information or incoming information to a line-level electrical signal, an amplifier that boosts the signals from line level to a stronger signal that drives the speakers, and speakers that convert the electrical signals into sounds. If a music system uses more than one audio channel (two for stereo, five or six for surround sound), each channel travels through separate wires from the program source to separate amplifiers and separate speakers. Many home entertainment devices, such as a table radio or a boom box tape or CD player, combine two or all three elements into a single box, but they are still sound-reproduction

systems that include at least one program source, an amplifier, and at least one speaker.

A home audio distribution system can carry either line-level signals to amplifiers in other rooms or amplified signals from centrally located amplifiers to remote speakers. Each approach offers its own advantages. Central amplifiers can be more economical, because a single amplifier can provide power for speakers in two or more rooms. On the other hand, when an amplifier is

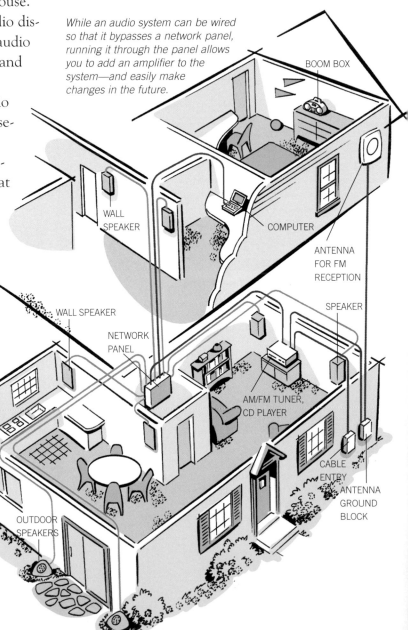

While an audio system can be wired so that it bypasses a network panel, running it through the panel allows you to add an amplifier to the system—and easily make changes in the future.

BOOM BOX

WALL SPEAKER

COMPUTER

ANTENNA FOR FM RECEPTION

SPEAKER

WALL SPEAKER

NETWORK PANEL

AM/FM TUNER, CD PLAYER

CABLE ENTRY

ANTENNA GROUND BLOCK

OUTDOOR SPEAKERS

in the same room as remote speakers, a listener can switch between music from the central system and programs from a radio, CD, or tape player, or a computer in the same room.

Remember that audio can move through a cable in only one direction. So every program source requires a cable (or a pair of cables for stereo) to the central distribution point, separate from the cable that provides audio to speakers in that room. For example, if there's no computer near the CD player and other program sources, it will be necessary to run a line-level audio cable from a computer in another room in order to play music files from the computer's hard drive or streaming audio from the Internet.

Each room served by the audio system must have speakers. A single speaker is adequate for a very small room such as a bathroom or a utility room, but most other rooms should have two or more speakers. Speakers can be built into the ceiling (see below) or wall (right) with wiring from amplifiers run inside the walls. Or they can be freestanding units connected to outlets or binding posts (see page 57) on wall plates.

If the amplifier is in the same room as the speakers, a separate volume control isn't needed. But if the speakers are powered from a central amplifier, plan to mount a volume control in the wall near the outlets or the speakers.

Outdoor speakers (like the "rock" at right) on a deck or in the back-yard are yet another option. The connection can be through audio outlets and a volume control behind a weatherproof cover mounted on an exterior wall. Speaker wires can be buried in conduit leading to strategically placed speakers along a garden path, or any other arrangement that fits your needs.

Think about your objectives as you plan your audio wiring. Do you want to provide seamless background music as people move from room to room? A system with central amplifiers and remote speakers is probably the best choice in this case. Or do you want to allow family members in various rooms to select their own music from a central source? In that case, place an amplifier in each room and distribute line-level audio.

It's not necessary to run audio cables through the central network control panel or to place the audio outlets in the same wall plates as data, video, and telephone. In many homes, the best locations for speakers or line-level audio connections may be on the opposite side of a room from the other network services. But it's usually easier to pull a bundle of wires through the walls at one time rather than pull cables individually. So routing the audio cables through the network panel and placing audio outlets near the others might be a good way to save some time during installation.

The alternative to running audio through the network panel is to install point-to-point audio wiring running directly from the program source selectors or the centrally located amplifiers to the rooms with the speakers in them.

Ceiling-mounted speakers are nearly invisible (left); wall speakers can also blend into their surroundings and typically offer better sound quality.

network control panel

The network control panel itself can be as simple as a sheet of plywood bolted to a wall (see page 96), or it can be a pre-wired cabinet (below) that mounts on the wall or gets installed between wall studs. All the data and video cables and all the new telephone cables will terminate at the panel, which contains the splitters, patch panels and terminal blocks necessary to distribute various signals throughout the house.

As discussed on page 19, the best place for the network panel in most homes is a central location (to minimize the length of cable and wire runs) in a dry, temperature-stable area like a closet or utility room. If there's an existing service entry or distribution point for telephone and cable TV wiring, consider placing the new network panel nearby.

If you choose to install PVC pipe for fishing cable between floors (see page 20), try to locate the network panel near the pipe. It's not necessary to bond the pipe to the network panel enclosure. Because the wires are low-voltage, they can be exposed as they run from the pipe to the panel.

Wherever the network panel is located, it should be mounted on a wall, at approximately eye level, with enough space around it to work comfortably. If there isn't already a light nearby, consider installing task lighting so that the equipment in the network panel is easy to see.

The network panel should also be close to at least one AC power outlet. Many video splitters, signal boosters, and other distribution devices require power connections, so it's common to mount some outlets on or in the network panel itself. (You can purchase an optional outlet strip made to fit a knock-out in the panel.)

If your current household network is a thicket of wires, you can appreciate the benefits of a network control panel that places all the connections in one spot. Designed to manage change, this type of box allows you to alter the function of lines by simply moving patch cords. While it looks a bit daunting, it is straightforward to install and assemble.

planning cable runs

Unless you are adding a network to a newly framed house or addition, running cable is the toughest part of installing a home network. You'll make the task easier by carefully working out your strategy in advance.

In general, the best routes for network cables are inside the walls to unfinished areas in the attic, crawl space, or basement. In a house with a crawl space or basement, most ground-floor cables can drop inside the walls from the outlets through the floor to the crawl space or basement. From there they can run along the joists and back up to the network panel. From the top floor, or when the house is built on a concrete slab, the best route is often upward to the attic, across the rafters, and down to the network panel or, in a multistory house, into a PVC pipe (see page 20) that leads to a panel.

It's usually easier to route network wiring through spaces inside walls that don't already have other services running through them. Electrical wiring, water pipes, and insulation can all create obstructions for network cables, so it's best to locate network outlets on inside walls, a foot or more from an AC outlet. When they're available, as-built blueprints or diagrams that show where other wires and pipes are located can be tremendously helpful, though don't be surprised if you find some installations that are not shown in the plan.

Closets are great for hiding cable runs between floors, especially when there's a space (such as another closet) above or below where the cables can continue their passage out of sight. A few wire wraps (page 52) will tidy up the bundle and keep cables from being snagged.

If it's not possible to run the wiring either up or down, consider a possible sideways route to another room, or run the wiring behind or along the baseboards or under the edges of wall-to-wall carpeting. Don't give up hope if there isn't an obvious route for cables from the network panel to rooms in the center of the house. One way or another, there's nearly always a path. Bear in mind, however, that the shortest route is not always the easiest.

A crawl space, basement, or attic allows you to spread your cable runs horizontally to reach each room from either above or below.

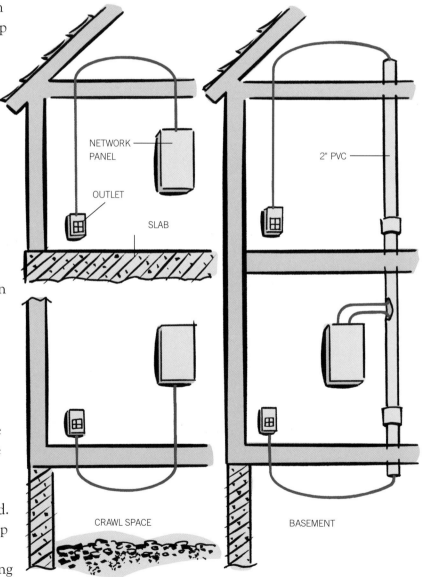

NETWORK PANEL

OUTLET

SLAB

2" PVC

CRAWL SPACE

BASEMENT

tools & materials

INSTALLING A HOME NETWORK REQUIRES TOOLS to cut openings, pull cables, attach connectors, install devices, and test the wiring. Many of these are the same simple hand tools used in general home improvement projects, but a few are specialty tools that are used only for data, telephone, and video cabling. ■ *As with most projects around the house, it's generally a mistake to cut corners on the cost of the tools you buy; well-made and well-designed tools are almost always easier to use. On the other hand, it's not always necessary to choose the most expensive professional-grade tools and test equipment, especially if they'll be used only a few times. Cable strippers, punch-down tools, and other specialized installation tools are all available in less costly versions that are entirely adequate for a home network project.* ■ *Even if you already have pliers and screwdrivers in your general-purpose toolbox, you can save a lot of time and trouble by assembling a kit for your network project. Some people like to use a tool belt (see page 44), but if you are running cables through a crawl space or other tight quarters, a handheld toolbag might be a better choice.* ■ *In addition to tools, a home network project requires a supply of cable, connectors, and mounting hardware. Most of these supplies are available at the same home centers and hardware stores that stock the installation tools.*

Although running cable is not a messy job, a drop cloth eases cleanup. In addition to assembling the tools you need, consider your own comfort and safety. For example, installing outlets means a lot of time spent kneeling. A pair of knee pads can make the task less wearing.

hand tools

Data, video, telephone, and audio wiring all carry low-voltage signals, so they don't require all the same precautions that are necessary for installing 120-volt electrical service. Nevertheless, it's worth spending a little more for tools with insulated handles so they'll be safe for electrical work in the future. For example, if all of your screwdrivers are insulated, you'll always be safe grabbing the one nearest at hand when making an electrical repair. Here are the hand tools you'll need for installing a home network.

LONG-NOSE PLIERS

These pliers are the best choice for grabbing individual wires inside a cable, for bending wires to hook them on screw terminals, and for reaching into tight places. Larger pliers are best for general use, but a smaller second pair can be handy for close work. Look for pliers with insulated handles that fit comfortably in your hand. Hold the tool up to the light to make sure the jaws fit together without gapping. Most large long-nose pliers include side-cutting blades inside the pliers' jaws.

GENERAL-PURPOSE STRIPPER

STRIPPERS

Wire and cable strippers come in many forms. A general-purpose stripper (above) will be needed if you have to run a 120-volt line to a network panel. A small stripper (right) is adequate if you are installing speaker wire or a few data cables. However, the best choices for data and video work are specially designed strippers like the cable stripper (below), which quickly removes the plastic cable jacket from CAT 5e cable, or the coaxial stripper (below right), which simultaneously makes the three delicate cuts necessary for stripping RG6 or RG6/U video cable.

SMALL STRIPPER

CABLE STRIPPER

COAXIAL STRIPPER

WIRE CUTTERS

A small wire cutter, also called a nipper (top right), is the best tool for cutting individual wires within a cable and for trimming loose ends. Larger cutters are better for cutting a whole cable at one time. They come in two forms: diagonal cutters (right) with short jaws and beveled cutting edges for close work, and side cutters, which are usually combined with lineman's pliers (below). Lineman's pliers can be useful for grabbing and holding cables. Be careful not to apply too much pressure when grasping a cable with any pliers—you might damage the individual wires inside the cable.

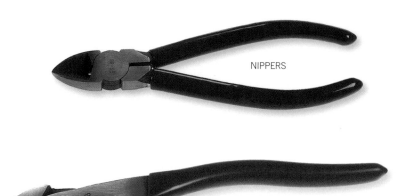

NIPPERS

DIAGONAL CUTTERS

LINEMAN'S PLIERS

SHOULD YOU INVEST IN A STRIPPER-CRIMPER?

Although expensive, this tool is handy should you need to make a number of long CAT 5e (or telephone) patch cords. It not only strips both data and telephone cables, it includes crimpers for their connectors. However, it takes practice to insert wires in the proper order and attach the connector correctly. Manufactured patch cords are reliable and available in a variety of lengths. Buying cables instead of making them yourself is the safest way to assure a functioning network.

PUNCH-DOWN TOOLS

Many telephone and data connectors use specially designed terminal strips into which wires are pressed. This is a convenient system for the connection of wires, because it eliminates the need to strip insulation. Some data and telephone connectors come with cheap plastic punch-down tools (above right). These are fine for connecting a few wires, but they do require the additional step of trimming the excess with a pair of nippers after the wire has been attached. For high-volume work, such as for a large terminal block in a control panel, a better choice is a spring-mounted punch-down tool (right). It automatically cuts off the excess as it punches a wire into place.

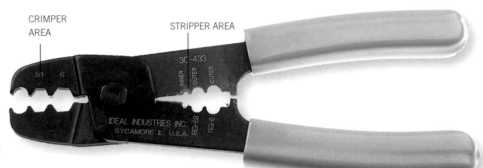

PLASTIC PUNCH-DOWN TOOL

SPRING-MOUNTED PUNCH-DOWN TOOL

F-CONNECTOR TOOLS

Every video cable (including the ones that run inside the walls) will require an F connector at each end. Attaching the connectors to the cables requires a special tool (right) that crimps the metal connector to the cable. Look for a tool designed specifically for attaching F connectors to RG6/U cable. An F-connector tool (below) has a threaded holder for the connector and a special screwdriver like hex socket tool for installing and removing F connectors in tight places.

CRIMPER AREA

STRIPPER AREA

HEX SOCKET

THREADED HOLDER

ELECTRICIAN'S TOOL POUCH

Unlike a typical carpenter's belt, with a hammer loop and nail pouches, an electrician's pouch is tailor-made for carrying the tools needed for wiring. This means a clip for your tape measure, a chain for electrical tape, and numerous compartments for pliers, strippers, and screwdrivers. You'll do a lot less searching in your tool bucket if you strap on one of these.

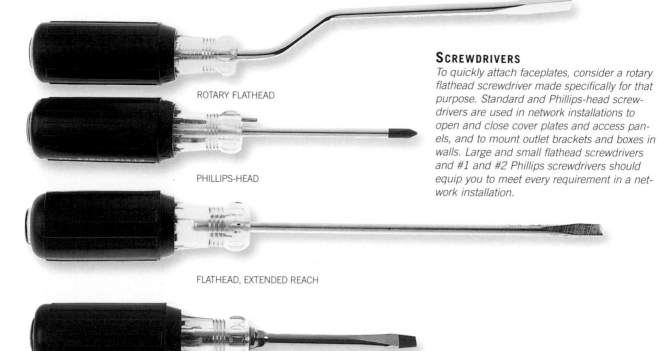

ROTARY FLATHEAD

PHILLIPS-HEAD

FLATHEAD, EXTENDED REACH

FLATHEAD

SCREWDRIVERS

To quickly attach faceplates, consider a rotary flathead screwdriver made specifically for that purpose. Standard and Phillips-head screwdrivers are used in network installations to open and close cover plates and access panels, and to mount outlet brackets and boxes in walls. Large and small flathead screwdrivers and #1 and #2 Phillips screwdrivers should equip you to meet every requirement in a network installation.

FISH TAPE

A fish tape is a long strip of flexible steel used to route cables inside walls, ceilings, and other hidden spaces. The tip of the tape is usually bent into a hook, so it's possible to grab onto a second tape from the other end of the cable run or attach the cable to the fish tape and pull it back through the walls. Look for a fish tape coiled inside a metal or plastic case that allows you to reel the tape in or out easily.

TAPE MEASURE

Whether you are marking to cut a hole for an outlet mounting bracket, establishing the height of the outlet plates above the floor, or simply rough-cutting a length of cable, you'll need a retractable tape measure. A 25-foot flexible metal tape measure is adequate for most wiring projects.

ELECTRICAL TAPE

It's better to tape a cable to the end of a fish tape than to tie it in a knot, especially when it must pass through a relatively small hole. Black plastic electrical tape is more durable and flexible than other household tapes.

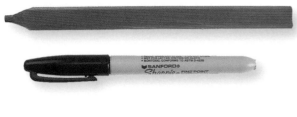

PENCIL AND MARKER

A carpenter's pencil (top left) won't roll away and seldom needs sharpening. Hold the pencil on edge and use the thin side of the lead. Have a permanent marker (left) on hand for marking wire cutoffs.

UTILITY KNIFE, DRYWALL SAW

A drywall saw (above) is ideal for cutting holes in plasterboard so you can fit mounting brackets or electrical boxes into the walls. It's also great for cutting access notches for horizontal cable runs. Scoring a drywall cutout first with a utility knife (right) makes for a smooth cut. The knife is also handy for cleaning out the openings.

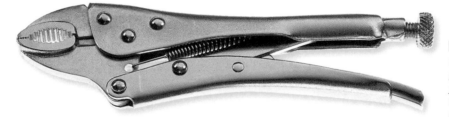

LOCKING PLIERS (VISE-GRIPS)

Locking pliers can hold a cable in place while you are soldering or when you are attaching the end of the cable to a plug or jack. Be careful not to damage the wire or cable by over-tightening.

HAMMER

For fastening "new work" boxes in place (see page 54), installing cable clips, and doing other general-purpose chores, a hammer is indispensable. If you are of slight build, buy a 13-ounce hammer; a 16-ouncer is suitable for people with a bit more upper-body strength.

STUD FINDER

Unless your network is part of a new construction project, you will need to locate the vertical studs inside the walls when you install network outlets. Electronic stud finders detect changes in the density of a wall and identify the location of hidden studs. Remember that network outlets should be kept away from the studs, not centered on them.

TORPEDO LEVEL

A small torpedo level (right) will help you mark for cutouts and check that boxes and outlets are plumb when you install them. It will also be handy if you decide to install a network panel or any other wall-mounted devices.

CABLE TESTERS

The football-shaped half of this two-piece tool sends a signal from one end of a data or telephone cable. The other half is shaped like a utility knife; it detects the signal at the other end. Testing a cable confirms that all of the wires inside are connected correctly to the outlet connectors at both ends and that none of them are broken or shorted. And once an installation is complete, a cable tester is the best way to identify a mislabeled cable. Look for a test set that can handle data and telephone cables. Each piece should have two sockets for the two types of connectors, or a short adapter cable that converts from one connector type to the other.

SOLDERING IRON

You'll need a soldering iron if your network includes high-level audio wiring. All the other cables in a home network—data, telephone, video, and audio speaker wiring—use punch-down or screw-down terminals. If you expect to use soldered audio connectors, look for a lightweight iron with a pencil or chisel tip and high-quality resin-core tin-and-lead solder.

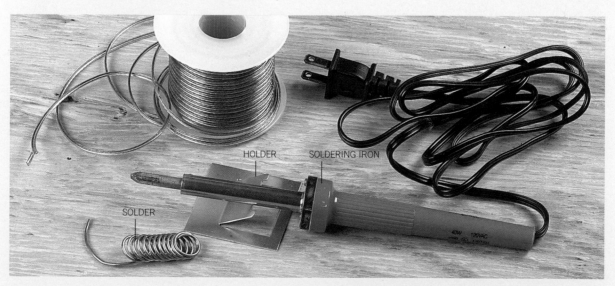

SOLDER   HOLDER   SOLDERING IRON

drills

Installing a network doesn't require a huge investment in power tools; running wire is unlikely to stress the tools, so you can get by with ordinary homeowner models. However, if you have to run cable through floor or ceiling joists or drill through hardwood flooring, or if you want tools that will be useful for general carpentry chores, invest in higher-quality models. While a ⅜-inch chuck is standard, a ½-inch chuck will accommodate bits with larger shanks.

POWER DRILL
Anytime a cable must pass between floors, it will be necessary to drill a few large openings. If you find yourself using a bit extension, piercing old wall studs, or drilling through concrete block, you'll need the staying power of a corded power drill.

SAFETY FIRST

Anytime you use power tools to drill or cut, protect your eyes with safety glasses and preserve your hearings with ear protectors. Running cable and installing outlets often involve a lot of kneeling; knee pads make the job much more pleasant. Optional protective gear includes gloves and a face mask—a must if you are boring into masonry.

CORDLESS DRILL
A battery-powered cordless drill is not only convenient, it has dual speed settings that let you use it as either a drill or a power screwdriver.

POWER SCREWDRIVER

This handy little rechargeable tool is ideal for fastening screws in outlet boxes. It can be a real time-saver if you are installing an expansive network.

DRILL BITS

For floor sills or other thick wood, use at least a ½-inch wood-boring bit (¾-inch or larger for multiple cables), with a spade-shaped tip and a hole near the end. The hole allows you to tie a string or light wire to the tip of the bit after it emerges through the hole and pull the cable back from the other side. A set of twist bits (right) is handy for installing network panels and other types of outlet boxes.

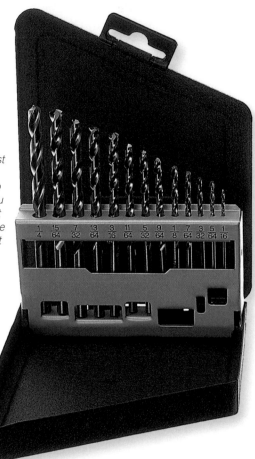

¾" SPADE BIT

½" SPADE BIT

ALLEN-HEAD WRENCH

SPECIALTY BITS AND ACCESSORIES

Most wood-boring bits are only about 6 inches long, which is often too short to reach through a floor. Use a foot-long drill bit extension to bore a deeper hole. Simply push a spade bit into the socket and tighten the Allen-head set screws. Or buy a long dual-auger bit—a hardworking tool that drills holes in a jiffy. When cables must pass through several ceiling joists, use a flexible fishing bit. It bends slightly to get into awkward areas and has a hole at the tip that you can use for securing and pulling cables.

DUAL-AUGER BIT

cables & connectors

A home network requires a variety of cables and connectors, each suited to the types of devices being connected. These include twisted-pair wiring for data and telephone lines, coaxial cables for video, and heavier wires for speakers and high-level audio. Each type of signal uses a different type of connector, so it's important to buy the right ones for each application.

DATA AND TELEPHONE WIRING

Data and telephone networks use cables that have several twisted pairs of wires inside a plastic sheath. The American National Standards Institute (ANSI) and the Electronic Industries Association (EIA) have established specifications for several categories of twisted pair cable, based on the amount of data that can pass through the cable, measured in bits per second. The CAT (category) number identifies the type of cable and its most common use. For example, CAT 1 cable is adequate for doorbell wiring and old-fashioned voice-quality telephone lines, CAT 3 (left) can handle voice and data up to 16 Mbps (millions of bits per second), and CAT 5 is good up to about 150 Mbps. In new-home construction the Federal Communications Commission (FCC) has specified CAT 3 wiring as the minimum acceptable quality for telephone service. Fast ethernet networks (which operate at speeds up to 100 Mbps) require CAT 5 cable or better.

CAT 3
CABLE

The best choice for both telephone and data wiring in a home network is CAT 5e (Category 5 enhanced) cable (above right). CAT 5e cables support higher bandwidth than CAT 5, with significantly better performance. CAT 5e is also quieter and less sensitive to interference.

CAT 5e costs a little more than CAT 5, but it's worth the extra expense because it will support the next generation of very high bandwidth data networks. CAT 5e cable contains four separate color-coded twisted pairs of copper wires. This means a single cable can carry up to four telephone lines or two data signals.

CAT 5e CABLE

Because you will use separate CAT 5e wiring for data and telephone lines, it's a good idea to buy boxes or spools of cable in two different colors. This will eliminate confusion when you're trying to figure out which cable is for voice and which is for data.

COMBINATION CABLE

Composite cable combines two CAT 5e cables with two RG6/U cables in a common sleeve. This is a great choice for a full-scale system that provides data, telephone, and video to every room. However, it's about 35 percent more expensive than separate runs of coaxial and CAT 5e, so ease of installation might be outweighed by cost.

VIDEO CABLE

A video signal contains a lot of information, so a video cable must be able to handle a much higher bandwidth than data or telephone cables. Video and cable modem services use a type of 75-ohm coaxial cable called RG6/U (right) that carries signals in a central copper wire surrounded by several layers of insulation and metal shielding.

RG6/U CABLE

The shorter video cables that connect TV sets, cable modems, and set-top boxes to wall outlets also use RG6/U.

DATA PATCH CORDS

Data patch cords connect computers, hubs, and other devices via the network outlets. If you have the connector tools, it's possible to make data patch cords out of the same CAT 5e cable that you use inside the walls, but it's seldom worth the time and trouble. Inexpensive premade cables are available in a wide variety of lengths and colors. As with the wiring inside the walls, make sure your cables meet the CAT 5e specifications.

SITE-MADE CAT 5e CORD

MANUFACTURED CAT 5e CORD

AUDIO CABLE

Household audio wiring comes in two forms: unshielded wire pairs that carry sound from a central amplifier to remote speakers, and line-level cables that carry programs from a CD player, digital audio server, tape player, FM tuner, or other program source to amplifiers located in the same room as the speakers they control. Line-level cables have two or four insulated 14-gauge wires wrapped with a sheathing. They are heavier and better insulated than speaker wires.

Many serious audiophiles believe that high-quality cables can make a big difference in the sound that comes out of the speakers. However, that quality comes at a price. Expensive interconnect cables might be practical between components in the same room, but long wiring runs throughout the house can be prohibitively expensive. And much of that expense will be wasted if those fancy wires are plugged into a pair of cheap speakers.

In practice, the quality of the sound produced by a speaker depends on a combination of factors, including the speakers themselves, the distance between the speakers and the amplifier, the diameter of the speaker wires, and, of course, the personal preferences of the listener. Using the most expensive wiring might not always be warranted, but it does make sense to look for wire designed for audio rather than using cheaper lamp cord.

For short runs (less than 50 feet), 16-gauge (16AWG) speaker wire is usually adequate. But if the total distance from the amplifier to the speakers is longer, or if you're using very low-impedance speakers (4 ohms or less), heavier 14-gauge wires are worth the added cost. (The lower the gauge, the thicker the wire.) Look for stranded copper cable, in pairs (for a single speaker), or use four-conductor jackets (for stereo pairs).

Line-level cables carry less power than speaker lines, so they must be shielded against interference from household 120-volt wiring, radio signals, and nearby electric motors. For home wiring, a cable with two separate shielded twisted pairs for the left and right stereo channels in a single jacket will save time and space during installation.

14-GAUGE CABLE

16-GAUGE

WIRE MARKERS

Wire markers provide a consistent method for identifying each of the cables in a network system. If every cable has the same unique number or letter-number combination attached at both ends, the next person who works on the network won't have to spend time using a signal tracer to find the right cable in a bundle of identical lines. Remember, that next person might be you!

Wire markers come in books of self-adhesive, preprinted numbers and letters that wrap around the ends of cables. To permanently affix a marker, use transparent plastic tape or, best of all, clear heat-shrink tubing. Don't try to economize with masking tape or other household tape that will turn brittle and fall off in a relatively short time—bear in mind that the wiring will be in place for many years.

WIRE CLIPS

Inevitably, some cable runs will be exposed, whether across ceiling joists, through crawl spaces, or along baseboards. You'll need a variety of clips to hold them in place. If you are planning a major project, consider investing in a specialty stapler designed for fastening wires. The staples are soft enough to conform to the shape of the cable without biting into it. Such tools are a little pricey but will vastly speed up the job if you anticipate running a lot of exposed cable. Other alternatives are metal or plastic clips that hammer in place. Select the right clip for the cable; options are available for phone, data, and coaxial cables.

WIRE WRAPS

Wire wraps are inexpensive plastic strips that hold bundles of wires or cables together. Bundling avoids the rat's nest appearance of many loose cables and keeps them away from locations where they might be snagged or tripped upon.

To wrap a group of cables, loop the strip around them, insert the pointed end though the hole at the other end, and pull it tight. If the strip doesn't feed through easily, turn the wrap over and try again.

If there's a loose tail at the end of the strip, trim it off with a wire cutter. It's not possible to undo a wire wrap after it has been assembled around a cable bundle; the only way to remove a wire wrap is to cut it.

Wire wraps are available with holes for wood screws or sheet-metal screws, and with separate adhesive mounting pads that hold a wire wrap to a wall.

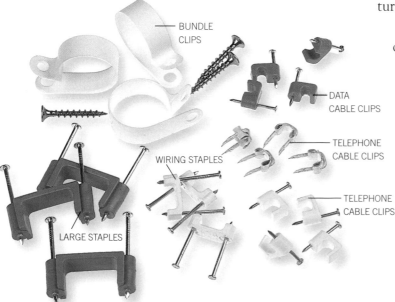

BUNDLE CLIPS

DATA CABLE CLIPS

TELEPHONE CABLE CLIPS

WIRING STAPLES

TELEPHONE CABLE CLIPS

LARGE STAPLES

wall outlets & surface-mounted boxes

In each room, the network wiring must terminate at one or more outlets, with appropriate connectors for data, voice, video, or audio. These outlets can be located in wall plates (right) similar to the ones that hold electrical outlets, or in small outlet boxes (below right) attached to the baseboard. Wall plates present a cleaner, more finished appearance, but surface-mounted boxes are easier to install and are fine in places that are hidden behind bookshelves, tables, or other furniture.

The most versatile wall plates and outlet boxes come with holes for snap-in connectors that can combine two or more types of network service into a single plate or box. This makes it easy to add or change the type of network service available at the outlet. If a box or plate has more spaces than you need, use blank inserts to fill the extras.

Other wall plates and surface-mounted boxes have specific connectors molded into their faces. These outlets are fine when only one or two types of network service are needed, such as cable TV or a telephone line, but they could make things more complicated when it's time to add another type of network service.

Wall-mounted telephones require a special type of wall plate (below) with raised rivets that fit

the holes in the back of the telephone set to hold it to the wall. Most wall phone plates contain only one jack, but special plates with one or two added jacks for an answering machine or modem are also available. Don't try to combine a wall phone outlet with other network services, because the plate will be hidden behind the telephone instrument.

This wall outlet setup accommodates three data or phone lines and two video lines, with a blank port available for future use. Each jack snaps into place. The faceplate and inserts attach to a mounting bracket or electrical box (see page 54).

Where only a single phone line is needed, a small surface-mounted box will do. It attaches to the baseboard with a double-sided adhesive pad or a screw.

mounting brackets & boxes

Wall plates for network wiring don't require the same kind of insulated mounting boxes used for electric outlets and switches (although it does no harm to use them), but they do need a box or bracket to which they can be fastened.

In new construction, use lightweight plastic boxes (right), attached to the studs before the wall material goes on. These come with nails for mounting on framing members. A plastic tab sets the box the right distance out from the stud to allow for ½-inch plasterboard.

Use remodel-type mounting brackets for installing outlets in existing walls. Both the boxes and the brackets have threaded holes that match the location of the mounting screws in standard wall outlet plates. (Unfortunately, these don't fit some brands of network faceplate that require a standard electrical wiring box. Check in advance.)

Surface-mounted outlet boxes (see page 53) attach to baseboards or other surfaces with wood screws, or with double-sided adhesive foam tape. If you are installing many such boxes, have extra screws and a supply of double-sided tape on hand.

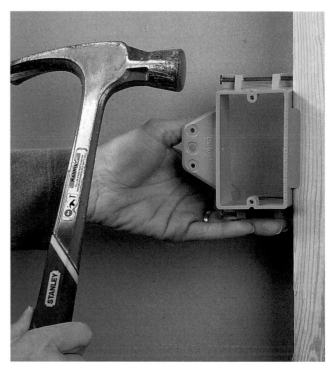

If you are adding a partition wall or finishing a new home or addition, you can use a "new work" box like the one shown above. Two nails (included with the box) fasten the box in place. With existing walls, first cut a hole and then place a remodel-type mounting bracket like the one shown below. As you tighten screws placed in opposite corners of the bracket, wings swing out to clamp the bracket to the wall material.

In addition to the remodel-type bracket shown at right, you can also purchase thin-profile and metal types (left). Extra screws and self-adhesive pads (above) are handy if you are installing several surface-mounted outlets.

connectors & jacks

Each type of network cable requires a particular jack in the wall outlets to suit the connectors that attach computers, TV sets, telephones, and other devices to the network. Computer data, telephones, video, and audio all use specialized connectors and jacks that have been designed for optimal performance. Consequently, you'll get poor results if you use an audio plug with a telephone, or a data connector for cable TV service.

As a side benefit, using a different type of connector for each service makes it easy to find the right jack at a glance, even if two or more services share a single wall plate.

DATA CONNECTORS

The standard connector for computer data in a home network is a type RJ 45 connector. RJ 45 jacks have eight conductors, with punch-down terminals. Many suppliers offer RJ 45 jacks in a range of colors, which make it easier to find the right one when you are plugging in a device. Some data jacks are labeled "CAT 5" or "CAT 5e," which can help distinguish them from similar telephone jacks.

TELEPHONE OUTLETS

Telephone systems use type RJ 11 connectors and cables to link telephone sets, modems, answering machines, fax machines, and other devices to wall outlets. RJ 11 jacks are narrower than RJ 45 data jacks, but they use similar internal wiring terminals. If you mount both data and telephone connectors in the same wall plate or surface box, use a different colored jack for each type of service.

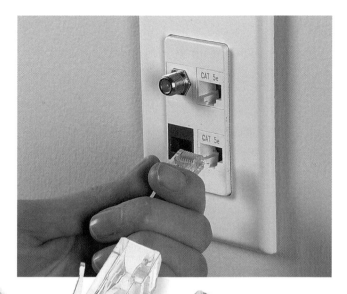

A data cable connector (known as an RJ 45) fits only data jacks.

Telephone cable connectors (RJ 11) can fit into a telephone jack or a CAT 5 or 5e jack, but they're not recommended for data lines.

VIDEO CONNECTORS

Video cables use threaded type F connectors, which provide continuous electrical shielding (by means of the braided layer) through to the jack. A second F connector inside the wall attaches the cable to the jack.

F connectors for video and cable modem signals are available in several forms. Some use twist-on compression rings to hold the connector to the cable, while others have a housing that is crimped permanently onto the cable.

The newest generation of F connectors, such as RCA's Centerpin type (right), eliminate the need to trim and strip the cable before you attach the connector—a difficult step unless you have a specialty stripper (see page 42) made for the job.

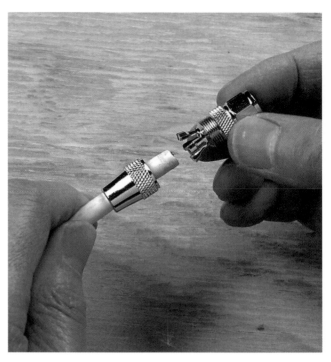

Some F connectors don't require that you strip the cable before adding the connector. These are more expensive but save time.

CHROMIUM TWIST-ON F CONNECTOR

CHROMIUM CRIMP-TYPE F CONNECTOR

BRASS CRIMP-TYPE F CONNECTOR

BRASS TWIST-ON F CONNECTOR

Several different types of F connectors are available, but all perform the same basic function—connecting video and cable modem devices.

(see page 42)

TIP: TIGHT SPOT?

Because video cables and connectors are inflexible and relatively long, it's often necessary to allow several inches of clearance around each socket. A right-angle video adapter can solve this problem when the outlet is located in a restricted space, such as on a wall next to or behind a bookcase.

SOLDERABLE
SNAP-IN
AUDIO JACKS

AUDIO JACKS

Audio jacks come in several forms, including binding posts for speaker wires (these have a twist ring that clamps the stripped end of the speaker wire), RCA jacks for cables leading to amplifiers, and jacks for banana plugs. Look for the type of connector that matches those on your speakers or amplifier.

RCA-TYPE
SNAP-IN JACKS

SNAP-IN
BINDING POST JACKS

SECURITY SYSTEM
DSL FILTER

PHONE/DATA
DSL FILTER

DSL FILTERS

DSL service utilizes the same wires for broadband Internet access and standard telephone service. The two operate independently, but an always-on DSL connection will sometimes add noise to the telephone line, which can interfere with modems, fax, and caller ID, and which creates a distracting "hash" sound on voice calls.

To eliminate this interference, connect a simple filter to every telephone set and other device that shares the line with the DSL modem. Most DSL service providers can supply these filters; they're also available at electronics supply shops and other telephone retailers. A security system requires a DSL alarm filter. Because the filter requires specialized testing equipment to make sure it has not compromised the effectiveness of the security system, it should be installed only by a licensed alarm service provider.

installing network wiring

WHEN THE INTERIOR SKELETON OF THE HOUSE IS EXPOSED—AS IN A NEWLY framed house or addition—installing network wiring is relatively easy. You'll have little difficulty drilling through joists and wall studs to place the cables in exactly the right place, without having to poke through invisible spaces with a fish tape. ■ With finished walls, the task is more demanding. You'll have to use some special tools and techniques to carve a route through walls, ceilings, attics, and crawl spaces—any cavity that gets your cable from point A to point B. ■ Start with the floor plan you created during the planning stage. It should identify the origin and destination points for each cable, the type of outlet at each end, and the approximate route between the two points. ■ Installing cables may not involve any heavy lifting, but it does sometimes require an assistant. In an old house, it's often necessary to have one person feeding cable into a wall and a second person pulling it through. An assistant may also be needed to snag a fish tape as it passes a tiny hole in the wall or to manipulate a second tape as you navigate cable through a particularly complex path. ■ The process begins with cutting holes for the outlets. Once the cable is run, the wiring is completed when you install the connectors and jacks.

Fireblock—a horizontal section of framing inside perimeter walls—can obstruct a cable run. If there is no way to go around it, cut into the wall and make a notch in the stud for the cable run. Have an assistant help ease the cable through the notch as you pull the cable.

getting started

Whether your goal is a simple link between two computers or an elaborate household-wide network, there are some general principles you should bear in mind before attempting to run the cable. They apply whether you are working with exposed framing or fishing cable through old walls.

WORK WITH THE FLOOR PLAN

Every network cable has an origin and a destination. Whether the network is a simple point-to-point (or point-to-multipoint) data system or a complex set of data, telephone, video, and audio hookups that run through a central distribution panel, every cable must follow a path from one room to another. Your floor plan should show each destination outlet in every room and the source at the other end of the cable. Whether or not you choose to use a central distribution panel, all the cables will run from some kind of distribution point to outlets in multiple rooms. Data cables will run from a network hub, telephone and video cables will originate at the service entry, and audio wires will extend from the main stereo system or the computer that acts as the audio server.

Once you've decided where each cable should begin and end, the next step is to find the simplest path. This takes some understanding of the way your house is constructed. Most framed construction uses 2×4 vertical studs to support the walls, with the centers of adjacent studs spaced 16 inches apart. (Less commonly, studs are installed 24 inches apart.) In older homes, the spacing of studs may be less consistent, especially when walls are covered with lath and plaster.

Think about the route of the cable as a combination of horizontal and vertical paths. If the control panel or distribution center is on the ground floor, it's often easiest to route the cable down from an outlet through the floor and then run it horizontally along the crawl space or basement ceiling joists and back up to the network panel (see page 39). Alternatively, the cables from each outlet can run through the attic or inside the ceiling or floor. Should you locate your network panel away from the attic or under-floor paths, installing a PVC conduit (page 20) will help you gain access to horizontal pathways.

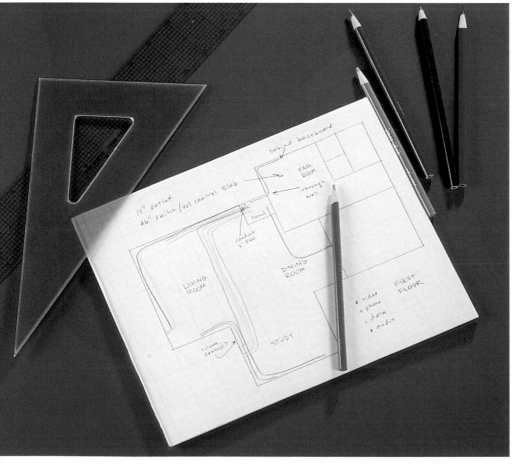

Draw a scaled plan to work out likely routes for your cables. Include the types of cable you will bundle together.

IF POSSIBLE, RUN CABLE IN A STUD SPACE SEPARATE FROM AC WIRING. IF THE LINES MUST SHARE A CAVITY, MAINTAIN 8" MINIMUM SPACING.

12" APART

NETWORK OUTLET

120-VOLT RECEPTACLE

KEEP A DEGREE OF SEPARATION

In order to prevent interference with the network signals and possible shorts from their crossing the AC power wiring, the network cables should be at least 8 inches away from electrical wires and 24 inches from motors and fluorescent lights.

Keep network outlets 12 inches or more from AC outlets. For example, if an AC receptacle is attached to a wall stud, place the network outlet close to the next stud rather than side by side. Unlike an AC outlet, whose connections must be enclosed in a box, a network outlet plate can use a lightweight mounting bracket located anywhere along a wall.

Position the network outlets the same height above the floor as the AC outlet boxes, typically 12 inches. In a kitchen, the best place for network and telephone outlets is generally on a wall above a counter rather than at floor level. If AC wiring passes through a hole in a framing member, drill a hole for the network cable at least a foot away. If the two types of cable must cross, be sure that they do not touch and that they cross at a 90-degree angle.

Stabilize the cables. Attach the network lines to framing with a cable tie, clip, or appropriate staples. Don't use a standard staple gun on data or telephone cables; the pressure from the staple as it comes out of the gun can crush the wires.

PERMANENT LABELING

Labels will help you keep cables sorted as you make your installation, and they'll be even more valuable in the future should you need to tie new devices into the network. Use ready-made self-adhesive labels (see page 52). To ensure they won't drop off later, add transparent tape or, even better, transparent heat-shrink tubing.

Labels held on with transparent tape.   Applying heat-shrink tubing.

HANDLING CABLE

It makes no difference whether you start at the outlets and pull the cables toward the network panel, or start at the network panel and feed cable to each outlet location. However, it's usually easier to feed cable downward through an access hole than it is to push it up. So the best approach is often to start at the top of the house and feed your cables toward the floors below. For example, if the network panel is in the first-floor utility room, feed the cables from outlets in the upstairs rooms down to the panel.

How long can a run be? Limit a single run of CAT 5e cable to 300 feet. While RG6/U can be run as far, if you split the signal more than three ways, you'll need to install an amp (see page 108).

Label both ends of every cable with the same unique number and keep a careful log of the numbers as you assign them. Even if you are pulling several cables together through the same pathway, each line should have its own number. Use a system that identifies the room where the outlet is

located and the type of service that the cable will carry. If you are pulling several cables at once, give each a number. For example, the two data cables that run from the network panel to the kitchen might be labeled as K1D and K2D. The video cable to the kitchen could be K3V. Make at least two copies of a wiring list like the one below showing the number and the end points of each cable. Post one copy on the wall next to the network panel and keep the other copy with the instruction manuals for your computer. Remember to note all changes on both copies whenever you add new network cables or change the existing services.

ROUTING CABLES BETWEEN FLOORS

As discussed on page 20, it can be an enormous aid to a network wiring project to install a 1½-inch

List each cable's type, origin, destination, and use. Assign each cable a code number. For example, "K2T" marks a cable running from the kitchen. It is the second cable in a bundle and is used as a telephone line.

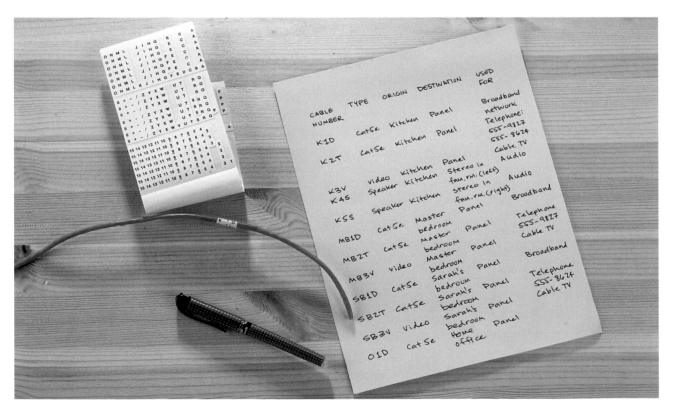

When two or more cables share a path, wrap the ends together with electrical tape to create a cable bundle and then feed the bundle through the walls at the same time. Most home centers sell CAT 5e of different colors. Use one color for data cables and another for telephones.

or 2½-inch PVC pipe to serve as a conduit between floors in a multistory home, with a break at each floor to run cables to their outlets. If a single conduit is not feasible, separate pipes for each floor are worth considering. During construction, it's often practical to place conduit pipes inside the walls. During a remodel, or when you are adding new network wiring to an old house, it might not be possible to find an inconspicuous

location for a single pipe all the way from the attic to the crawl space or basement. But there may be a usable route next to the wall inside a closet, in the laundry room, or in some other out-of-the-way location. If possible, the pipes should emerge close to the network panel.

Conduit pipe isn't absolutely necessary, but it will make it easier to run your cables now and add new cables in the future. As technology changes and new types of wiring become standard, the conduit you install today will provide a route for new cables as they are needed.

One other good practice when you're running network cables is to always leave yourself a "messenger line." When it's time to thread the cables through the wall or drop them through the conduit pipes, attach nylon cord or strong fishing line to the end of the cable bundle. Once you've run the cable bundle to its destination, untie this line and secure at each end a large nut that will make it easy to find. The messenger line will be there waiting the next time you need to pull a new cable along the same path.

WORKING SAFELY WITH LOW VOLTAGE

The low-voltage signals carried on data, telephone, video, and audio wiring present no danger of injury. Should you happen to be holding a phone wire or two when the phone rings, you'll feel it, but the biggest likely danger posed by a shock from a ringing telephone line would be if you jumped up and bumped your head because the mild shock surprised you.

running cable in open framing

Install network cables after the other household services are in place, including roughed-in household wiring, plumbing, and heating/air conditioning. This ensures that your network wiring won't be in the path of another service. It also allows you to position network wiring an adequate distance from the electrical wiring (see page 61) and reduces the chance of damage to your network as the other services are installed.

Choosing the pathway for your cable is pretty straightforward when the framing is exposed. In fact, you may be choosing among several equally efficient pathways. Generally, the easiest path is from above or below. You'll create openings through the sole plate or the top plate of the wall framing by drilling ¾- to 1½-inch holes (depending on whether you are running one cable or bundling several together). Be sure the holes you cut don't pass all the way through a finished ceiling or floor on the next level; instead use the space between the floor and the ceiling as a path to the nearest interior wall. Because perimeter walls are obstructed with insulation and sometimes fireblocks, interior walls are generally the best choice for routing cables.

In rare situations, pathways above and below may not be available; you will have to make horizontal runs through the framing (see opposite).

Always select the option that involves the least hazard for the cable. For example, it's better to run cable along the face of ceiling joists in an attic rather than perpendicular to them. If you have to go perpendicular, run the cable along the base of the rafters, where it is less likely to be snagged or crushed.

Because the spaces inside walls are so much easier to reach during new construction, there is all the more reason to consider your future network cabling needs. Even if you don't need them right now, think seriously about installing two CAT 5e cables, two video cables, and perhaps two audio cables at every outlet. If you ever use even one of these extra lines in the future, you'll more than recoup the cost of the extra materials in saved labor.

This simple installation in an interior wall shows a bundled cable (left) emerging from the sole plate. Notice that the network outlet bracket is at least 12 inches from the electrical box. Network cables and household wiring lines have separate access holes.

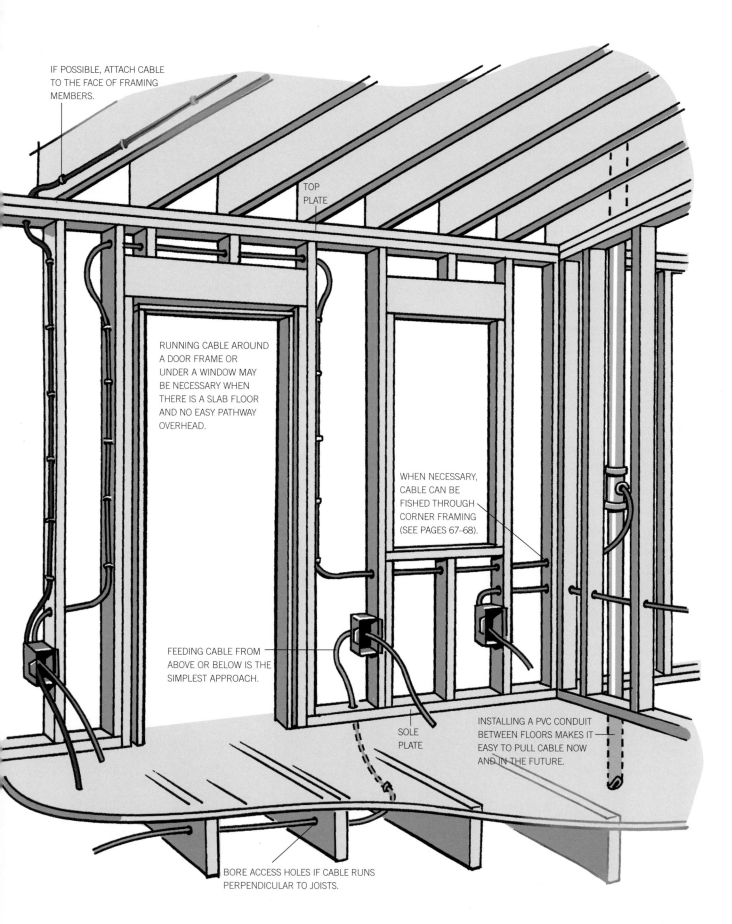

IF POSSIBLE, ATTACH CABLE TO THE FACE OF FRAMING MEMBERS.

TOP PLATE

RUNNING CABLE AROUND A DOOR FRAME OR UNDER A WINDOW MAY BE NECESSARY WHEN THERE IS A SLAB FLOOR AND NO EASY PATHWAY OVERHEAD.

WHEN NECESSARY, CABLE CAN BE FISHED THROUGH CORNER FRAMING (SEE PAGES 67–68).

FEEDING CABLE FROM ABOVE OR BELOW IS THE SIMPLEST APPROACH.

SOLE PLATE

INSTALLING A PVC CONDUIT BETWEEN FLOORS MAKES IT EASY TO PULL CABLE NOW AND IN THE FUTURE.

BORE ACCESS HOLES IF CABLE RUNS PERPENDICULAR TO JOISTS.

PULLING CABLE

As a general rule, try to drill holes in framing members as close to the center of the wood as possible. A hole through the face of a 2 × 4 should be at least 1½ inches from either edge. An alternative to drilling through the studs is to cut a small notch on the edge of each board to provide space for the cable. Secure the cable with a staple or strap and cover it with a protective nailing plate.

In most houses, the cable path will need to pass through one or more access holes before it reaches the network panel or distribution point. Starting at one end of the run, feed the cable through one access hole at a time, taking care as you go to smooth any kinks or tangles. Do not attempt to drag the cable through several holes at once; doing so risks damaging the cable.

Repeat the process, one stage at a time, until the cable reaches its destination. Allow about 2 extra feet of each cable at each end. This will provide enough slack to connect the outlets without the need to hold them right against the wall during installation.

Whether working in open framing or with finished walls, have one person to pull cable and another to guide the bundle into the access hole. The job will go much more easily, and there will be less chance of damage to the cable.

COAXIAL CABLE

CAT 5E CABLE   CAT 5E CABLE

BUNDLED CABLE

KEEP IN TOUCH

Pulling cable between rooms or floors is best done by two people (above), and you can help matters go even more smoothly by equipping yourself to communicate easily. A pair of walkie-talkies, or even a cell phone in tandem with a cordless telephone, will help coordinate the process.

ESSENTIAL CABLE-RUNNING SKILLS

FASTENING BOXES OR BRACKETS
Nail mounting brackets to the framing, at least 8 inches away from any AC wiring and 12 inches from an electrical outlet. Position the bracket 12 inches above the floor—roughly the height of a hammer stood on its head.

DRILLING ACCESS HOLES
Bore access holes through the sole plate or top plate for pulling cable to another floor. Use a ¾-inch bit for one or two cables, or a 1-inch bit for a bundle of four cables. (If installing a standard electrical box, break out the restraining tabs before pulling cable.)

FISHING CABLES THROUGH CORNERS
At corners, drill two holes to access the cavity between the studs. Push in fish tape or a bent piece of coat hanger to help pull the cable through. If you will be running your cables through such a corner from an adjacent hole in the framing, enlist a helper to smoothly feed the cable through as you pull from the other end.

THREAD CABLE ONE STUD AT A TIME

To protect the cables, thread the bundle through one access hole at a time. Pull the entire cable run through before moving on to the next stud. (You can always back off a bit if you find you've pulled the cable too far along.) Add protective nailing plates wherever the cables run through a framing member.

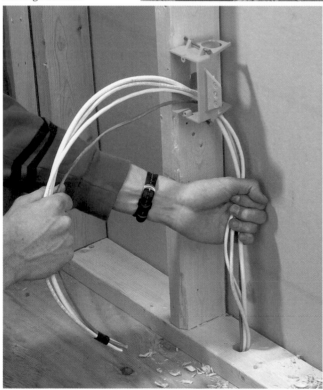

ALLOW EXCESS CABLE AT THE OUTLET

At the end of each run, leave 2 feet of excess cable protruding from the bracket. This will give you plenty of cable to work with when you are attaching jacks. The excess can later be pushed into the wall cavity—a bonus for the next person who works on the outlet.

COIL AND TUCK CABLE

To keep cables from being damaged when the drywall is installed, coil the ends and tuck them into the box.

COVER BOX OPENINGS

If your walls will be spray-painted or textured, keep your cables from getting gummed up by covering the face of the box with painter's tape. Cut the tape away after the drywall has been taped and painted.

SECURE ALL VERTICAL RUNS

Stabilize vertical runs of cable with the appropriate staples or clips. In the example shown, speaker wires leading to an outlet for a wall-mounted speaker are being secured with clips.

MAXIMUM CABLE BENDS

There are limits to the flexibility of network cabling, so be careful during installation. Category 5e (CAT 5e) cable can safely bend to a 1-inch radius, while stiffer coaxial cable should not bend to more than a 2½-inch radius. If either type of cable kinks, cut the kink out and discard it. Do not attempt to splice either type of cable.

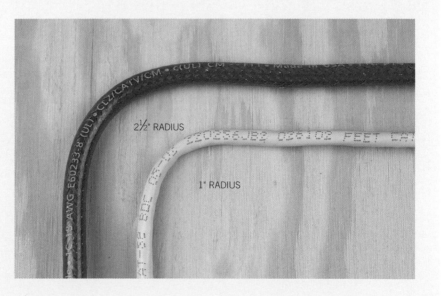

2½" RADIUS

1" RADIUS

installing cable in finished rooms

When adding network outlets to a finished room, you can't simply choose a location for the outlet and drill some holes for the cables. Instead, you'll have to ponder the hidden cavities within your walls and ceilings with an eye toward finding the least troublesome path from point A to point B. You'll likely have to drill finder holes to probe hidden spaces, manipulate fish tapes through invisible passages, and, with some trial and error, finally run the cable where you need it to go. At times, pulling new cables through an old house can give new meaning to the phrase "You can't get there from here."

The least troublesome approach—and the most visible—is to run cable along the base shoe to surface-mounted outlet boxes attached to baseboards. In inconspicuous locations such as behind sofas or beds, surface installations may be an acceptable option.

A related approach is to pierce a perimeter wall and run your cable outdoors. This is especially useful, for example, in bypassing the second story of a three-story house. Telephone installers have used this technique for years.

The neatest and most permanent approach, however, is to run the cables within the walls. With careful planning and a bit of luck, running cable in this manner sometimes goes surprisingly smoothly. The illustration opposite shows the most common avenues for running cable in a house with finished walls.

EXPLORE ALTERNATIVES

There are two sides to every wall, floor, and ceiling. Look for unfinished spaces in adjacent rooms before you cut holes in the wall where the outlet will be located. Anytime you can run the cables through a closet, utility room, crawl space, attic, or basement, there is one less hole to be patched in the finished wall. If you have forced-air heating and air conditioning, consider using the air return ducts for running cable.

Whenever possible, avoid placing outlets in exterior walls. In addition to insulation, perimeter walls often have horizontal members called fireblocks between the studs, about halfway between the floor and the ceiling. These make it difficult to pass cables.

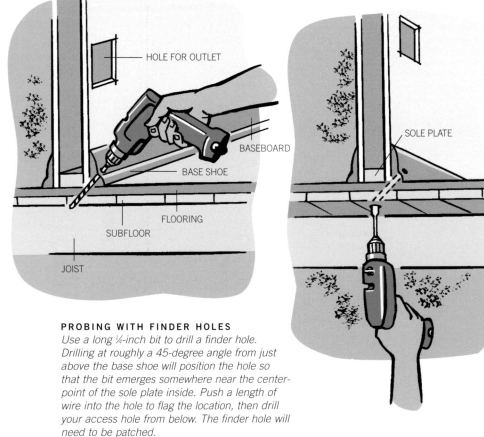

PROBING WITH FINDER HOLES
Use a long ¼-inch bit to drill a finder hole. Drilling at roughly a 45-degree angle from just above the base shoe will position the hole so that the bit emerges somewhere near the center-point of the sole plate inside. Push a length of wire into the hole to flag the location, then drill your access hole from below. The finder hole will need to be patched.

HOLE FOR OUTLET

BASEBOARD

BASE SHOE

FLOORING

SUBFLOOR

JOIST

SOLE PLATE

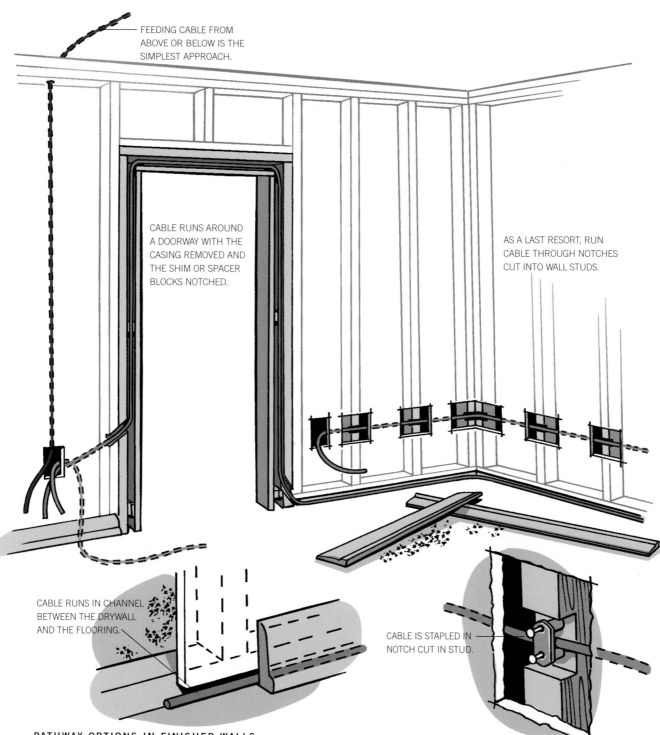

FEEDING CABLE FROM ABOVE OR BELOW IS THE SIMPLEST APPROACH.

CABLE RUNS AROUND A DOORWAY WITH THE CASING REMOVED AND THE SHIM OR SPACER BLOCKS NOTCHED.

AS A LAST RESORT, RUN CABLE THROUGH NOTCHES CUT INTO WALL STUDS.

CABLE RUNS IN CHANNEL BETWEEN THE DRYWALL AND THE FLOORING.

CABLE IS STAPLED IN NOTCH CUT IN STUD.

PATHWAY OPTIONS IN FINISHED WALLS

The simplest way to run cable through finished walls is to cut openings at the top or bottom and fish the cable from the attic (as shown by the red cable) or feed it from a crawl space or basement below (green cable). The task is more difficult where there is no access from above or below—for example, in the first story of a two-story house built on a slab. In such a case you may have to remove the baseboards to hide cables or run the line around a door-way (blue cable). Although it involves a lot of patching, lacing the wiring through multiple access holes cut at each stud (orange cable) is another way to make a horizontal run. Use protective nailing plates (page 68) wherever a nail might pierce a cable.

CUTTING HOLES IN PLASTER AND LATH

It is nearly impossible to cut neat holes in plaster and lath, but here is a method that helps. Begin by applying masking tape to the cutout area and scoring along the cut line with a utility knife. Drill access holes and use a saber saw or keyhole saw to complete the cutout.

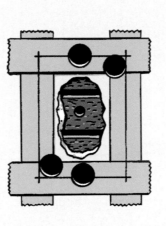

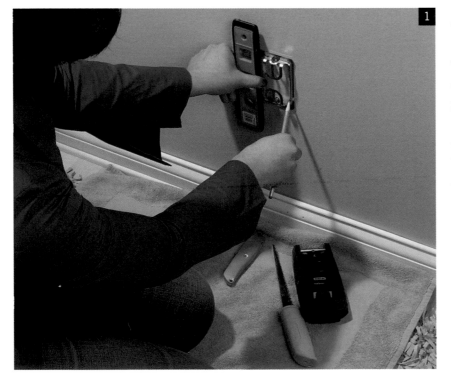

The best way to deal with fireblocks is to avoid them, either by installing the network outlet below the fireblock, when there is a possible cable path down through the floor, or by using an interior wall for the outlet. If you have no alternative, find the fireblock, cut into the wall, and notch the fireblock (see page 59).

PREPARING FOR OUTLETS

Since you will be installing your outlets in holes cut through the existing drywall or plaster, you'll need to use so-called old-work brackets or boxes with flanges that grip the bracket in place (see page 54). Installation is quite easily in drywall, but it's a bit more challenging with plaster and lath.

Generally, the bottom of each bracket should be about 12 inches above the floor, but you'll want to match the height of any existing electrical outlets for a consistent appearance.

Prepare the work area by laying down a drop cloth; cutting holes through either drywall or plaster can be a messy job.

1 Mark for the bracket
Using an electronic stud finder, locate the studs in the wall on either side of the spot where you want your outlet. Staying at least 4 inches away from the studs, mark an opening slightly larger than the size of your

bracket. Use a level to make sure that the hole you are marking is plumb.

2 Score the cutout

Score your pencil marks with a utility knife to ensure a neat hole. You want the cutout to be large enough to allow you to push the bracket in but not so large that you'll have to patch wide gaps that won't be covered by the outlet faceplate.

3 Cut the opening

Starting at one corner, punch the tip of the drywall saw through the scored line, tapping on the handle with the palm of your hand. The saw is designed for this puncturing action. Saw along each side. Use the bracket to check the opening. If the hole needs enlarging, shave its edges with a utility knife.

4 Install the bracket

Pull your cable all the way through the opening before installing the bracket. The bracket will only get in the way if it is fastened in place before the cables are installed. Feed the cable through the bracket and push it into the cutout. The type of bracket shown here has two flanges that bend back behind the wall material; other types have winged screws that you tighten until you feel the wings draw up against the wall material (page 54).

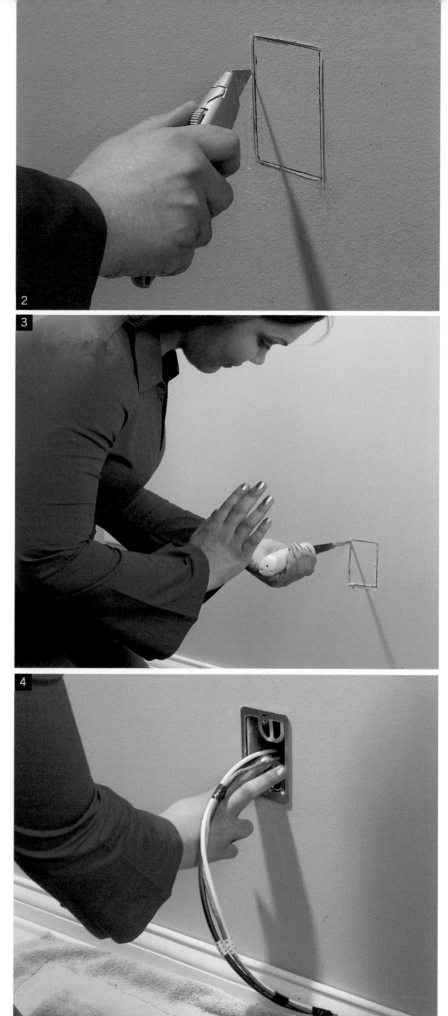

RUNNING CABLE BEHIND BASEBOARDS

Although cable can be clipped or stapled along the top edge of the baseboard, the wood trim might be put to better use hiding the network cables. By prying away the baseboard, you can create a channel in the wall material. A variation on this technique can be used to route cable around a door (page 71).

1 Score along the baseboard

Often, paint will pull off the wall as a baseboard is pried away. To avoid needless paint touchups, use a utility knife to score along the top of the baseboard. Also score the junctions where the baseboard meets other trim, as at corners and doorways.

2 Pry off the trim

With a pry bar and a couple of stiff putty knives, carefully remove the trim along the cable route. Use side-cutting pliers to remove the finishing nails from the back of the trim. Grab each nail with pliers and twist. The nail will pull out, head and all, leaving the trim face unmarred. If you've been able to remove baseboard and base shoe in one piece, nip off the finishing nails holding the shoe in place.

3 Make a channel

If you are lucky, you may find a ready-made channel between the bottom of the drywall and

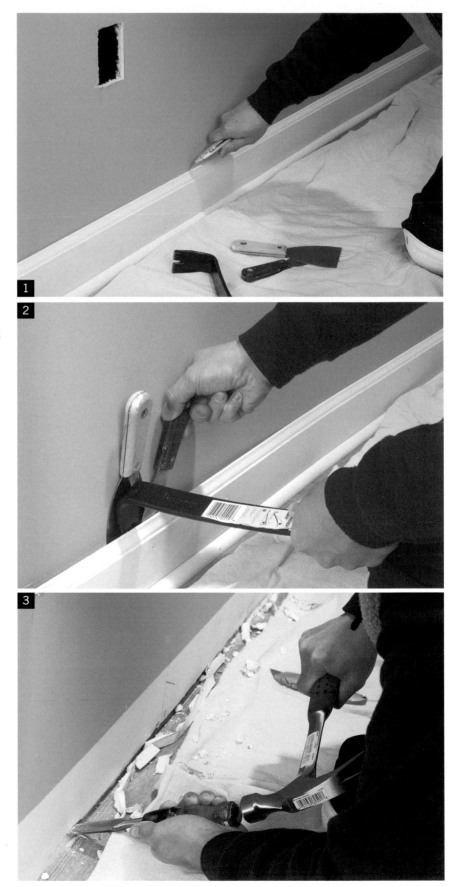

the flooring. More typically, you'll have to use a utility knife, hammer, and chisel to remove enough material from the bottom edge of the wall to make room for your cables.

4 **Run the cable to the opening**
Drill into the wall cavity just above the 2   4 sole plate at the bottom of the wall framing. Push the cable into the hole and up toward the opening. Reach into the outlet hole and pull the cable through.

5 **Place the cable**
Leave at least 2 feet of cable protruding from the outlet hole. Push the cable into the newly created channel at the base of the wall, fastening it in place with clips.

6 **Replace the baseboard**
Replace the baseboard and base shoe. Nail them in place with 6d finishing nails, being careful to avoid piercing the cable. Set the nail heads with a hammer and nail set. Fill the resulting indentations and any remaining nail holes with tinted putty.

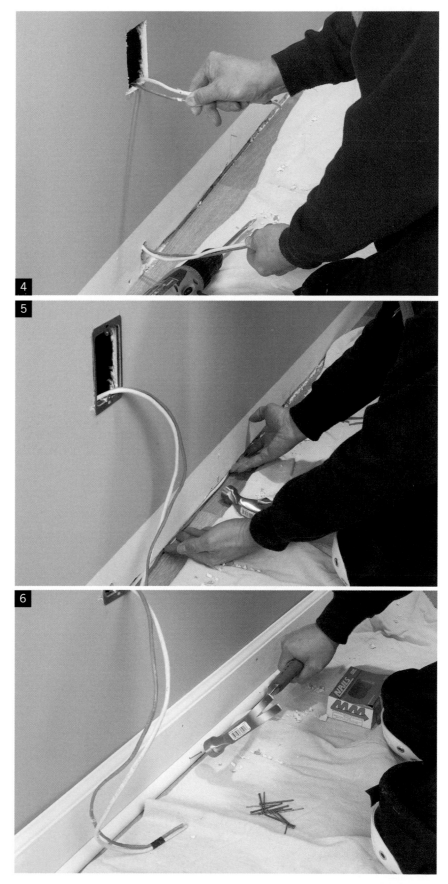

MAKING PATHWAYS THROUGH WALLS

Exhaust all other possibilities before assuming you need to make a lot of holes in your walls to run the cables. To route cables inside the walls up from the basement, use a drill with a bell-hanger bit or an auger bit with an extension shaft (page

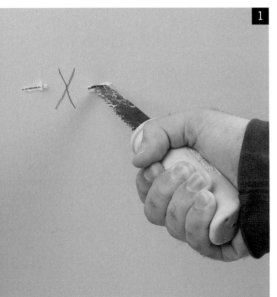

49) to drill through the sole plate. If cable will be fished up from below, drill down through the sole plate so that your holes can be hidden by the baseboard. Do everything you can to limit later patching of the walls.

Sometimes, however, the only way to get the cables where you need them is to cut some extra holes so you can notch framing members to create a pathway. If you use this technique, plan a route that crosses the least number of studs to limit the amount of patching that you will have to do.

1 Locate the stud

Using an electronic stud finder, mark the locations of the studs to be crossed by your cables. The stud finder will give you only the general location of the stud. To precisely find the edges

of the stud, push a drywall saw into the wall about 2 inches from your mark. Saw on each side until you feel the blade hit the wood.

2 Cut an opening

Using a torpedo level as a guide, lightly mark the outline for a hole in the drywall. The hole should extend about an inch beyond the edges of the stud and be about 2 inches high. Score these lines with a utility knife and cut the opening with a drywall saw.

3 Notch the studs

Using the drywall saw or a keyhole saw, make two cuts through the stud ½ to ¾ inch deep. Chisel out the waste to create a shallow notch in the front of each stud. This allows the cable to pass across the framing member with-

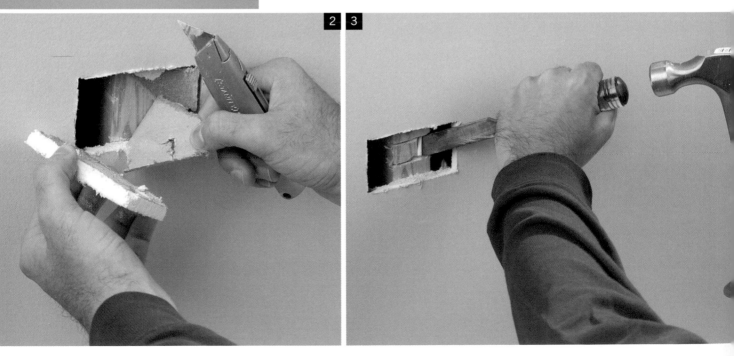

out creating a bulge once the drywall is been repaired.

4 Run the cable

Push a fish tape from the opening for your outlet toward the first stud to be crossed. Hook this first fish tape with a second one fed from the cutout at the stud. Then pull the second tape to the outlet hole. Attach the cable and pull the entire run through the notch in the stud. Secure it loosely with a staple to hold the cable in place. When you are done running the cable, nail in each staple.

FISHING AND PULLING CABLE

In places where the cable will travel through the cavity of a wall or some other covered or enclosed space, use a fish tape to reach from the access hole at one end to the outlet hole at the other. Have a helper on hand so that one person can feed the fish tape into the cavity while the other person tries to snag it with a second tape. Small hands may be able to reach in and grab the tape.

Once you've successfully fished tape into the outlet hole, attach the cable to the end of the fish tape, using electrical tape. Your helper can then pull

While it takes some doing, one fish tape can be used to hook the end of another inside a wall. You can then pull the second tape through, attach the cable, and pull it to its destination.

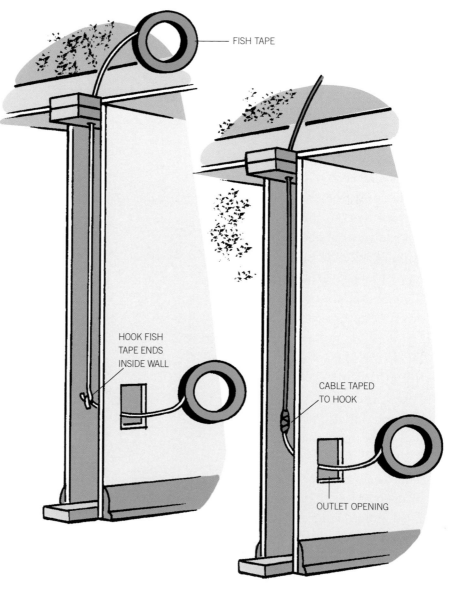

FISH TAPE

HOOK FISH TAPE ENDS INSIDE WALL

CABLE TAPED TO HOOK

OUTLET OPENING

Wall covering provides an opportunity to neatly disguise access holes. By carefully peeling back the covering before cutting the hole, you can create a flap that can be glued back in place after the access hole has been patched. Use a razor blade or a utility knife to cut a flap in the paper. If it doesn't come loose easily, try soaking it with warm water. Use masking tape to fasten the flap away from the work. After the wall has been repaired, use wallpaper paste or water-soluble white glue to fasten the wall covering back in place.

the tape back until the cable emerges. In some circumstances, such as when you are running cable down from an attic, you'll find it easiest to thread the fish tape down from above and use it to pull back either a second fish tape or a nylon string. This can then be used to draw the cable down from the attic.

FILLING HOLES AND REPAIRING DRYWALL

After the cables are in place and the wall outlets are wired, you may have to patch and paint a number of holes in your walls. There may also be a few gaps or open spaces that need to be filled around your mounting brackets.

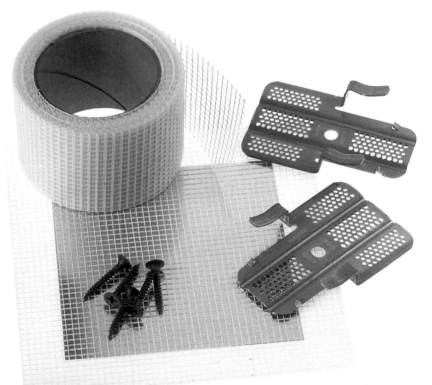

Patching materials and hardware specially made for the purpose can speed up the patching process. However, the final feathering and smoothing of the joint compound are the keys to an invisible patch.

Small holes and gaps are easy to patch with quick-drying joint compound or Spackle. Once it has set, use a drywall taping blade (see step 5 on page 80) to knock off any ridges. To reduce dust, use a dampened abrasive sponge to smooth the repair.

To fill a larger hole in drywall, use the procedure that follows.

1 Prepare the patch

Cut a patch from a new piece of drywall. To avoid gaps in the joints between the patch and the opening, make the patch somewhat larger than the original hole.

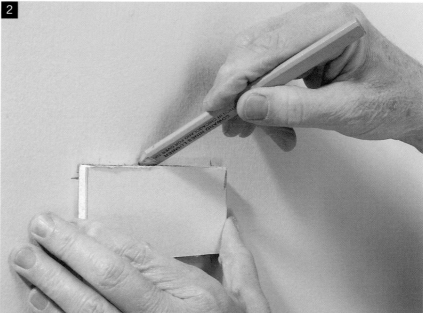

2 Mark a cut line

Use the new patch as a template to draw a cut line around the hole in the wall. If possible, set a corner of the patch in the hole so you'll have to enlarge only two sides.

3 Enlarge the opening

Using a drywall saw, expand the hole to fit snugly around the patch by cutting along the new outline. Be careful to hold the cable out of the way as you cut.

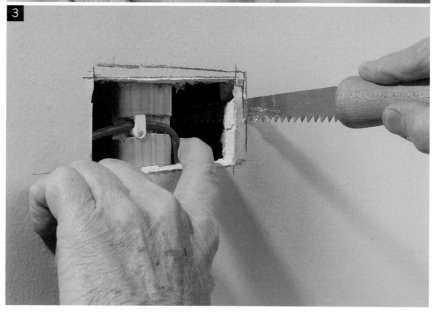

4 Fasten the patch

If the hole exposes a stud or a joist, fit the patch into the hole and attach it with drywall screws or nails. If there is no exposed wood on which to anchor the patch, use patch clips like those shown on page 78.

5 Apply the first coat

To avoid hairline cracks, cover the seams with adhesive mesh tape. Use a taping knife to cover the mesh with a smooth layer of joint compound. Work the compound to completely fill the seams. Leave the surface as smooth as you can.

6 Apply additional coats

Add a second coat of joint compound over the patch with a wide drywall knife. Hold the knife at a 45-degree angle to the surface and pull the compound in the same direction that the tape runs. The joint compound should extend 2 or 3 inches beyond the edges of the tape, with the edges feathered to make a smooth transition to the wall surface.

7 Smooth the patch

When the joint compound is dry, use your taping blade to knock off any ridges. To reduce dust, use a dampened abrasive sponge to smooth the patch. Hold a light close to the wall to reveal any flaws; touch them up as necessary. Prime and paint.

ROUTING CABLE THROUGH AN UNFINISHED ATTIC OR BASEMENT

When network cables need to run across the floor joists above an unfinished basement, drill holes in the joists to provide a path. When the cables are to run parallel to the joists, hold them in place with clips or staples.

As a general rule, it's always best to run cables either parallel or perpendicular to the house's framing rather than just stringing them diagonally across the basement ceiling or an attic floor. Even in an unfinished space, aim for a neat installation. Remember that network cables should not be bent in too tight a radius (see page 69), so let them follow a wide curve when they change directions.

In an attic, it's important to avoid creating a tripping hazard, especially near the stairway or access hatchway. Install your cables away from these areas. If it's not possible to feed the cables through holes in the joists, use wire staples or cable ties every 12 inches or else run them across the tops of the joists with guard strips along each side of the cable.

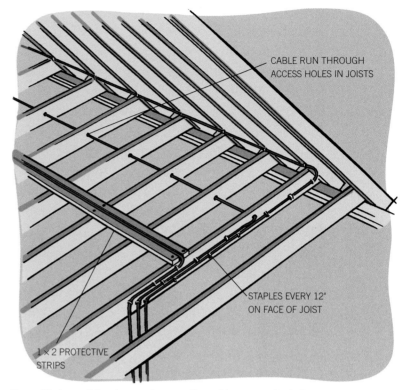

If an attic is used for storage, be sure the cables are protected. Ideally, cable should be stapled along the faces of joists (not the tops). Cable runs perpendicular to the joists should have guard strips or be tucked out of the way at the base of the rafters.

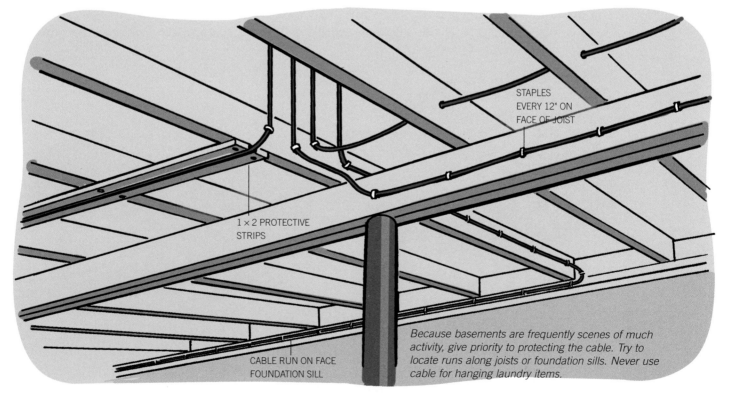

Because basements are frequently scenes of much activity, give priority to protecting the cable. Try to locate runs along joists or foundation sills. Never use cable for hanging laundry items.

connecting outlets

Each type of network outlet uses a different connector. Carefully follow the installation instructions supplied with your connectors; a single wire in the wrong place can make the whole system fail. A miswired connector can also be extremely difficult to trace.

CONNECTING DATA JACKS

The standard plugs and jacks used in computer networks follow the RJ-45 standard for modular data jacks. They're part of a series of "RJ" (registered jack) specifications established by the Federal Communications Commission (FCC) to define the most common connectors used in telephone and data devices. RJ-45 was originally an American standard, but it's now accepted around the world.

RJ-45 plugs and jacks have eight conductors, numbered (as you're holding the jack with the snap-in clip down) from 1 through 8, left to right. Remember that the jacks are wired from the back, so the numbering appears to run from right to left when the jack opening is toward you.

CAT 5e cables and RJ-45 connectors contain eight conductors, organized into four twisted pairs. Each pair includes one wire with solid-color insulation and the other with alternate stripes of that color and white. So it's common to refer to each pair by the color of the insulation—"the orange pair," "the green pair," and so forth. A data network connection uses only four of the eight wires, so the remaining wires of a CAT 5e

cable are available for a second data circuit or for two two-wire telephone lines.

Making things a bit more confusing than they ought to be, there are two different color codes for attaching wires inside a four-pair cable to an RJ-45 connector: T568A and T568B (see below). If you have old CAT 5e wiring in your home, it may use the T568A code, but for new installations T568B has supplanted T568A. Both codes work equally well, but it's essential that the connectors at both ends of a cable be configured the same way so that all the pins on the connector at one end are wired to the corresponding pins at the other end—pin 1 to pin 1, pin 5 to pin 5, and so forth. Choose one code and use it for every outlet in the house.

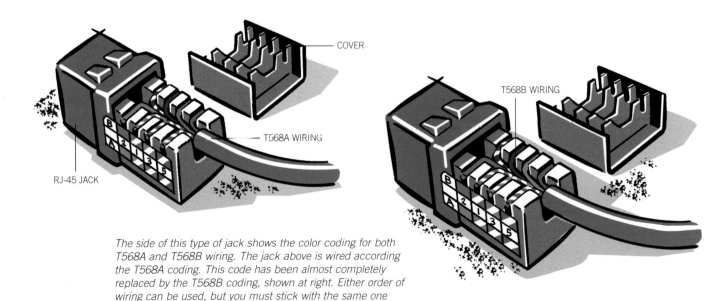

COVER

T568A WIRING

RJ-45 JACK

T568B WIRING

The side of this type of jack shows the color coding for both T568A and T568B wiring. The jack above is wired according the T568A coding. This code has been almost completely replaced by the T568B coding, shown at right. Either order of wiring can be used, but you must stick with the same one throughout your network.

RJ-45 DATA OUTLETS

The RJ-45 jacks used in wall outlets, surface-mount boxes, and network panels all have eight punch-down insulation displacement contact (IDC) slots that hold the eight wires of a CAT 5e cable. Many RJ-45 jacks come with a disposable tool that is generally adequate for forcing the wires into the IDC slots. However, a separate spring-mounted punch-down tool will make the job easier and faster, especially if you are dealing with a large number of connections, as in a network panel.

To attach CAT 5e cable to an RJ-45 outlet, follow these steps:

1 Strip the jacket

Make sure the cable is marked with a code number that identifies its use in your network (see page 62). Use a cable stripper to remove about 2 inches of the jacket from the end of the cable.

2 Separate the pairs

Pull apart the four pairs of wires, but do not untwist the individual pairs.

3 Insert the cable

Follow the instructions provided with the RJ-45 connector to route the pair of wires closest to the back of the jack over the correct IDC slots. As you position the wires in their slots, be sure the cable jacket extends into the jack. You may have to give the back pairs a twist or two so they are wound together within ½ inch of their punch-down connection. None of the internal wires should be exposed when the jack is fully assembled.

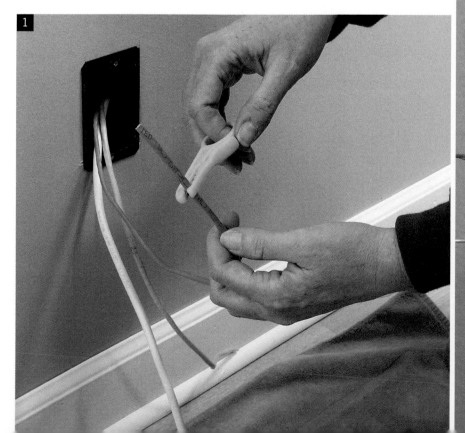

4 Punch down two wires

Use a punch-down tool to push the first two wires into the IDC slots. If you are using a spring-loaded punch-down tool, the tool will automatically cut off any excess wire ends. Make sure the tool is held so that the cutter blade is on the outer edge of the jack

5 Complete the wiring

Repeat the process for the three remaining wire pairs. Confirm that each wire is in the correct location according to either the T568A or the T568B color code, whichever you are using. If you're using a disposable punchdown tool, use a pair of wire nippers to remove the excess wire. If the RJ-45 connector includes a cover, place it over the connector, as described in the instructions supplied by the manufacturer.

6 Install the outlet plate

With the type of plate shown, the jacks are snapped in and then the plate is attached to the mounting bracket. Afterwards a faceplate is added. If you are using a snap-in outlet in a modular outlet plate, follow the manufacturer's instructions to insert the outlet into the plate. Don't mount the outlet plate to the wall until you have attached all the cables that will run to the outlet.

An RJ-11 jack is very similar to an RJ-45 jack, but it is coded differently. Its dust jacket is smaller because it protects fewer wires than that of the RJ-45 jack.

DUST JACKET

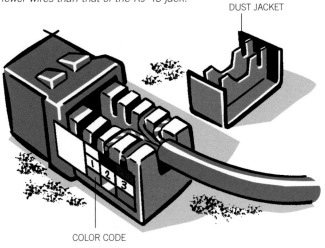

COLOR CODE

A modular jack lets you connect more than one device to the same outlet. The type shown above, for example, could accommodate a phone, an answering machine, and a fax machine.

TELEPHONE OUTLETS

Telephone sets, fax machines, modems, and other devices that connect to the worldwide public telephone system all use RJ-11 connectors. RJ-11 plugs and jacks are slightly smaller versions of RJ-45 connectors. An RJ-11 jack has space for six conductors, but most telephone cables have only two or four wires, so the plugs often have only two or four pins.

The original color code for telephone wiring dates back to the days when telephone companies used four-wire or six-wire cables for residential service. You will still see red, green, yellow, and black wires and terminals inside older telephone outlet blocks. When you use CAT 5e cable for telephones, the colors are different, so it's necessary to use a different color code. The table below shows how to translate from the old to the new color code.

Note that the wiring starts in the middle of the connector and works outward. The two center wires carry one line, and the next two carry the second line. The two remaining wires inside a CAT 5e cable are not connected to the telephone outlet. When you install a CAT 5e cable on an RJ-11 jack, either cut the wires off flush at the point where the cable enters the connector, or wrap them around the cable jacket. Don't forget to label the cable before you close up the outlet.

PIN NUMBER	OLD COLOR CODE	NEW COLOR CODE	TELEPHONE LINE
1	White	Green/White	Spare
2	Black	Orange/White	2
3	Red	Blue	1
4	Green	Blue/White	1
5	Yellow	Orange	2
6	Blue	Green	Spare

TELEPHONE PAIRS IN AN RJ-45 CONNECTOR

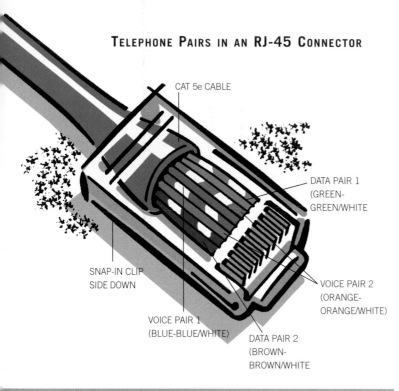

CAT 5e CABLE

DATA PAIR 1
(GREEN-
GREEN/WHITE)

VOICE PAIR 2
(ORANGE-
ORANGE/WHITE)

SNAP-IN CLIP
SIDE DOWN

VOICE PAIR 1
(BLUE-BLUE/WHITE)

DATA PAIR 2
(BROWN-
BROWN/WHITE)

To connect an RJ-11 outlet to a CAT 5e cable, follow the instructions on pages 83–84 for installing RJ-45 jacks. The manufacturer's instructions provided with the jacks will show which IDC terminal corresponds to each pin.

Because a telephone line uses only two wires, it's easy to send more than one telephone line through a single cable. If both lines will go to a two-line telephone set, use the modular cable supplied with the telephone.

OUTLETS FOR WALL TELEPHONES

Many wall telephones use a special outlet plate with two raised rivets to physically support the telephone. Two keyholes on the base of the telephone fit over the rivets. When the telephone set is mounted on the wall plate, either the RJ-11 connector on the telephone fits directly into the socket on the wall plate, or a short cable supplied with the telephone plugs into the wall outlet.

Because the wall plate is hidden under the telephone, it's not practical to use the same plate for data, video, or audio wiring. And because a wall phone is typically located between 4 and 5 feet above the floor, a loose wire running down the wall wouldn't be desirable. Most network outlet plates should be closer to the floor, where they are out of sight and pose less risk of tripping someone when cables are attached.

When a CAT 5e cable carries telephone service, only the blue-blue/white or orange-orange/white pair is used (above). Wall phones require a special mounting plate (left) with two raised rivets to hold the telephone in place. A short patch cord clips into the phone and into a jack in the mounting plate.

USING THE SAME CABLE FOR DATA AND TELEPHONE OUTLETS

It's best to run separate cables for data and telephone service, but when you want to add another telephone line to a location where a data outlet is already in place, it's significantly easier to use the spare wires in the existing cable than to pull a new cable.

As discussed on page 50, CAT 5e cable contains four twisted wire pairs. Since a data circuit uses only two of those pairs (see opposite), the other two pairs may well be available for this additional network connection.

This is practical only when the household network uses the same central distribution center for both data and telephone wiring. If the data and telephone wires terminate in different locations, don't try to work with a single cable.

To add a telephone outlet to an existing data outlet, or a new data outlet to an existing telephone outlet, follow these steps:

1 Detach the outlet
Remove the outlet plate from the wall, or remove the cover from a surface-mount box. Separate the cable and the connector from the wall plate or box cover.

2 Open the connector
Cut the cable as close to the jack as possible. Loop it in a loose knot to ensure that the cable doesn't slip back into the wall cavity. Pry the dust cover off the IMC terminals inside the jack.

3 Remove the wires from the jack
Use a pair of long-nose pliers to remove the wires from the jack. Grasp each wire and pull it up from the jack.

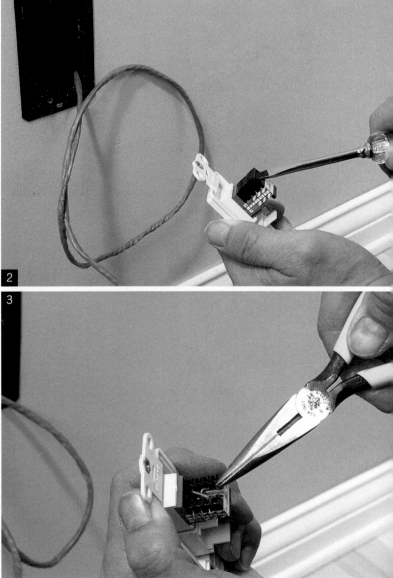

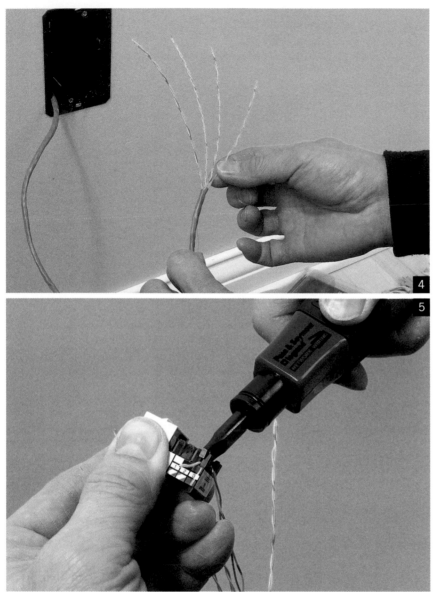

4 Separate the four pairs

Strip about 5 inches of the outer jacket away from the end of the cable (see page 83). Separate the four twisted wire pairs, but do not untwist the individual pairs.

5 Connect the brown pair

Use a punch-down tool to connect the blue pair of wires to pins 3 and 4 of the RJ-11 (telephone) jack. Connect the solid blue wire to pin 3 and the blue-and-white wire to pin 4. If your punch-down tool doesn't cut off the excess wire ends automatically, trim them with a pair of wire cutters.

6 Complete the wiring

Connect the remaining wires to the RJ-45 (data) jack, using either the T568A or the T568B standard. (Use the same wiring standard adhered to throughout

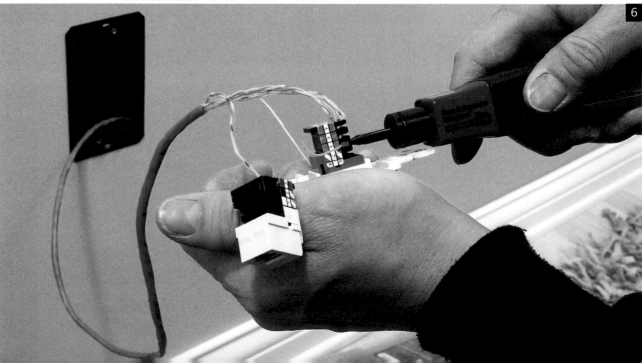

the rest of your network.)
If necessary, cut off the excess wire ends.

7 Seal the wires

Replace the dust covers over the IMC terminals on both jacks. Wrap the exposed wires with electrical tape. Label the data cable and the telephone cable where they branch from the CAT 5e cable.

8 Replace the outlet

Reassemble the wall outlet plate or the surface-mount box. If the plate or box cover doesn't have a spare opening for the new jack, replace it with a new piece that has the additional opening.

9 Make final connections

At the other end of the cable, connect the blue wire to the red terminal in the distribution panel for the telephone line; connect the blue-and-white wire to the green terminal. Then connect the remaining wires to the data distribution panel according to the color code used in your network.

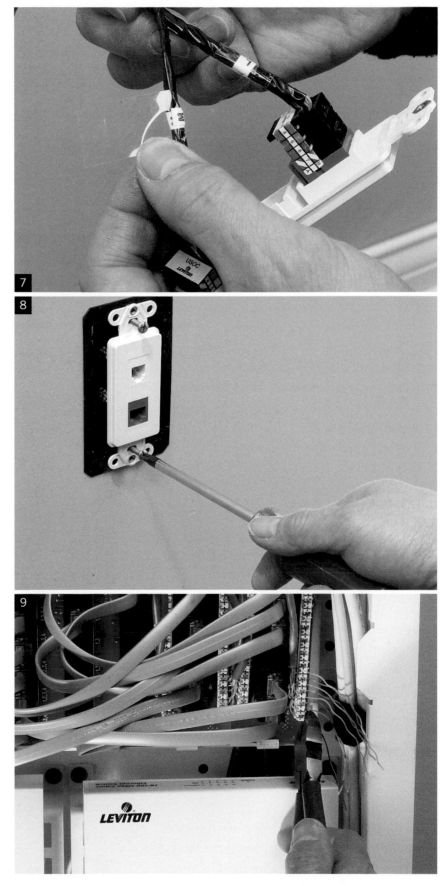

VIDEO OUTLETS

Video cables are extremely sensitive to interference from nearby radio transmitters, electric motors, and other sources. In order to minimize such interference, video cables and connectors maintain a continuous shield around the central copper wire. That is why the video outlets in network wall plates have F connectors (see page 56).

To install a video outlet on a wall plate, you will need to attach an F connector to the RG6/U cable and plug that connector into the mating jack inside the wall plate. F connectors come in several forms, each with a different method for attaching the connector to the cable. Most use some variation on the process of stripping the cable, inserting the connector over the center wire, and crimping the sleeve of the connector around the shield. Manufacturers provide detailed instructions for their particular designs.

In addition to the crimping tool that compresses the shell around the cable, look for the type of F connector tool that holds the plug on a threaded extension (see page 44). The added bulk of the tool makes the connector much easier to handle while you're inserting the cable.

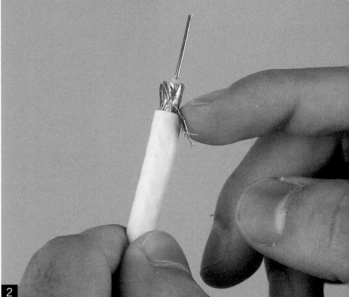

1 Strip the cable
Strip coaxial cable as shown, using a stripping tool, the stripping teeth on a coaxial crimper, or, trickiest of all, a utility knife. Even with a coaxial stripper, it takes a knack to get this step right; practice on a scrap of cable. Strip the cable so there is about ¼ inch of the braided shield and at least ¾ inch of cleanly stripped copper wire.

2 Peel back the braided shield
Carefully bend back all the steel braiding against the end of the cable sheathing.

3 Place the F connector
Push a crimpable F connector onto the cable, making sure the turned-back steel braiding slips into the connector. The white insulation that

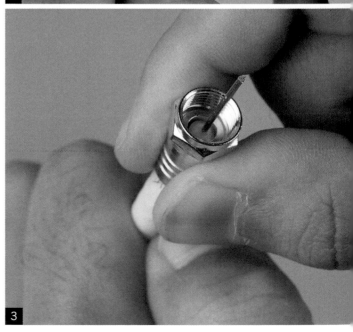

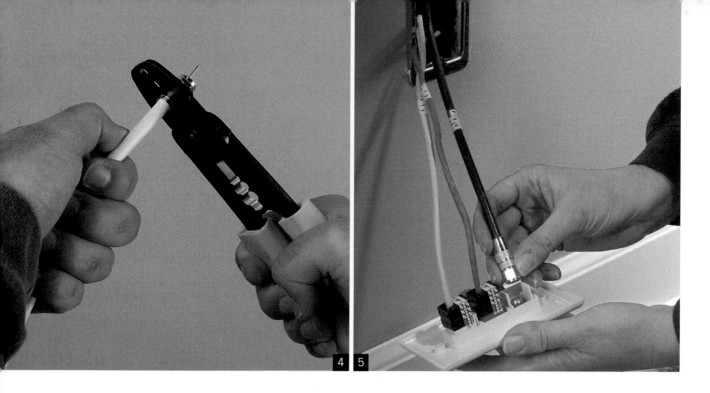

surrounds the copper wire should be pushed all the way into the connector.

4 Crimp the connector
Crimp the F connector in place using a crimping tool. Give the connector a firm tug to confirm

that it is fastened. Trim the center copper pin so it protrudes ⅛ inch beyond the connector.

5 Attach the cable to the back of the jack
Once the F connector is attached to the cable, twist it onto the threaded back of the jack.

NO STRIPPING REQUIRED

One alternative to the strip-and-crimp method is the RCA centerpin design. Although more expensive than standard connectors, these don't require a special stripper or crimper. During installation, you first trim off the cable squarely, then push on the connector cap until ½ inch of cable shows. Use pliers to push on the other half of the connector, pressing the six prongs evenly into the insulation. Finally, pull the cap forward and thread it over the prongs.

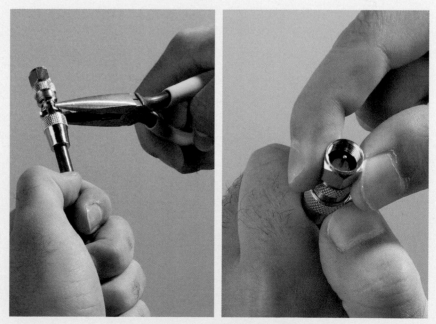

HIGH-LEVEL AUDIO CONNECTORS

The common connector for high-level audio is called an RCA plug, even though this type of jack is made by many manufacturers. RCA jacks on wall plates come in two forms: solderless connectors for CAT 5e cable and connectors with solder terminals for shielded audio cable.

Solderless RCA jacks are intended only for very short cable runs, such as the cable that connects the audio from a TV set to an amplifier a few feet away. Don't try to use them with the longer cables that connect an audio system from room to room; they'll add environmental noise to your music.

Use shielded cables and connectors with solder terminals for room-to-room audio distribution. Unfortunately, many of the most widely available RCA connectors for modular wall plates use solderless connectors, so they're not appropriate as part of a home network. Separate outlet plates with soldered terminals are a better choice.

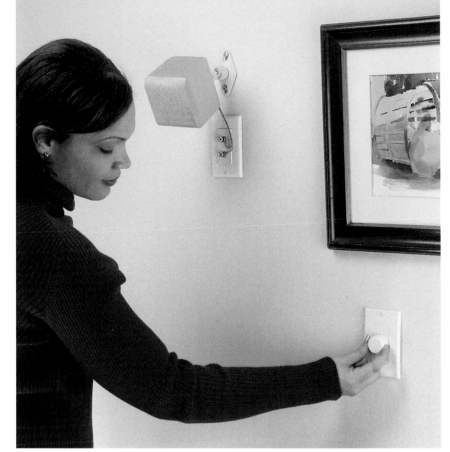

The volume of audio originating from a tuner, stereo, or cable source in another room can be adjusted with a remote volume control (also see diagram opposite).

SPEAKER TERMINALS

The ideal location for speakers depends on the size and shape of the room, as well as on the arrangement of furniture, windows, fireplace, and other features within the room. For serious listening, a room should contain two speakers for stereo, or at least five for surround sound. Stereo speakers should be located along the longer wall of the room, facing the area where listeners will sit. In spaces

Some audio jacks have pins to which speaker cables are soldered. Strip an inch of speaker wire, twist it, thread it through the pin, and then twist it in place. Heat the pin first, then apply a touch of rosin-core solder to the wire.

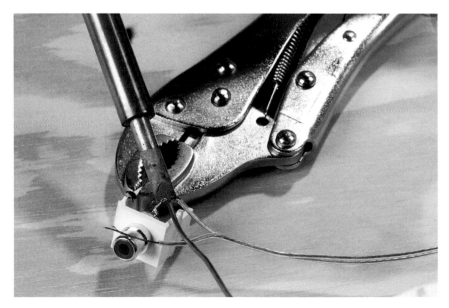

where the audio system is used for casual background listening, a single speaker may be adequate.

Every speaker requires a pair of wires from an amplifier. In a room with two speakers, the speaker terminals can be combined on a single wall plate about halfway between the two speakers, or placed on separate plates close to each speaker. The choice is a trade-off between convenience during installation and appearance.

While it's not absolutely necessary, a volume control that regulates the sound levels of both speakers is a convenient addition to the system. The volume control can be built into the wall or placed in a box on a tabletop or bookshelf between the speakers.

Most speaker outlets use binding posts that accept bare wires, spade lugs, banana plugs, and pin plugs. Each binding post uses a set screw to secure the audio distribution wiring, so the only installation tool required is a screwdriver.

To install a wall-mounted volume control, run the speaker cables inside the walls to the volume control location, and run separate cables from the volume control to each pair of speaker terminals, as shown below. If you're working in a finished room, it's best to place the speaker outlet wall plate directly below the volume control so that you don't have to run the speaker wires through vertical studs inside the wall. If that's not an option, cut a small hole in the wall at each stud and feed the wires through a notch in the stud. As an alternative, consider running the speaker wires down through the floor or up through the ceiling, and back to the outlet plates.

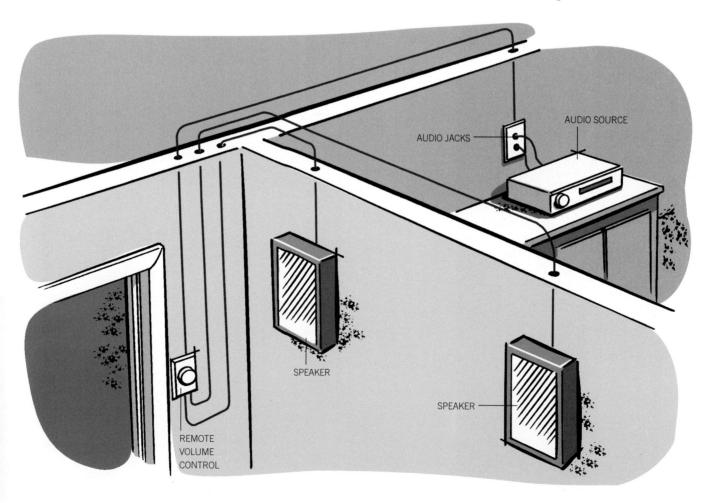

AUDIO JACKS

AUDIO SOURCE

SPEAKER

SPEAKER

REMOTE VOLUME CONTROL

A homemade panel like this one is an affordable option for modest-sized networks. While convenient, the modular systems that place everything inside a single package are actually sometimes a bit less flexible, since they don't always allow you to assemble components from more than one manufacturer.

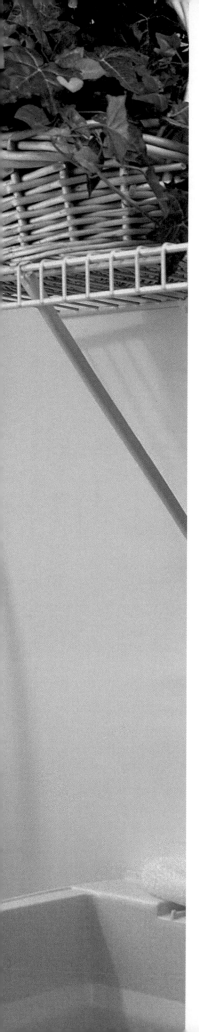

installing a network control panel

A NETWORK PANEL IS THE INTERFACE between the services in your network and their connections to the outside world. It's also the place where those services are routed to outlets throughout the house. ■ Whether or not the service entries and distribution points connect in a single control center, you're going to need a hub of some kind for each type of service. ■ The deluxe approach is the so-called home-run network, with data, telephone, and video outlets in every room and all the cables running through an off-the-shelf network panel. But such a system is only one option. If you simply want to share an Internet connection with two or three computers, there's no need to replace the existing telephone and video wiring or add a network panel. A simple point-to-point wiring system may be entirely adequate. ■ In this chapter you'll see how to install network hubs and connect incoming data, telephone, and cable and satellite TV services through those hubs. You'll also learn how to bring together those various services at a single control center.

build your own network panel

Modular network panels that combine all the network distribution services into a single enclosure are convenient and relatively easy to configure, but they're not absolutely necessary. Particularly if your network will only tie together your computers, you can build a network panel for yourself and save a lot of money in the process. Other types of network components for phone, audio, or video service can also be added, as shown in the panel at right.

On the 14 pages that follow, you will see how to assemble such a panel. In the photos on these pages, all of the network components are attached to a plywood backing mounted on the wall. Alternatively, you could organize your system on shelves or an equipment rack.

Then, beginning on page 110, you'll find a brief summary of how to achieve similar results using a manufactured modular network panel.

ASSEMBLING A DISTRIBUTION CENTER FOR NETWORK DATA

The network panel for computer data should have at least three components: a set of RJ-45 outlets connected to the CAT 5e cables from each room, a network hub where data moves from one network device to

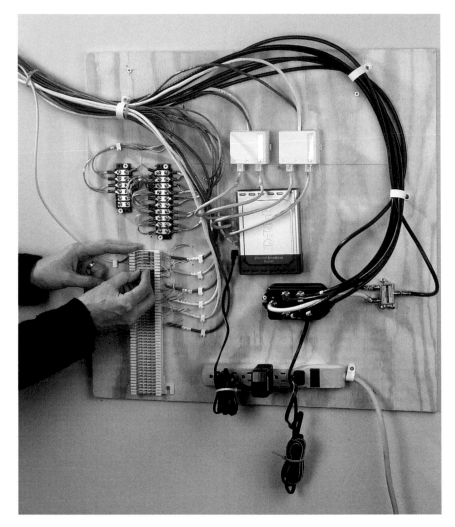

another, and a router that exchanges data between the local network and the Internet. The hub and router are often combined into a single package that performs both functions.

CABLE TERMINATION All of the CAT 5e cables from network outlets throughout the house terminate at the control panel. To connect these cables, attach one or two rows of surface-

mount RJ-45 outlet boxes to your plywood backing (above, right). Each surface-mount box can contain one or two outlets. Connect each data network cable to one of the RJ-45 connectors. Be sure to follow the same color code (T568A or T568B) on both ends of each cable. As you work, identify the opposite end of each cable on the cover of the box where it terminates.

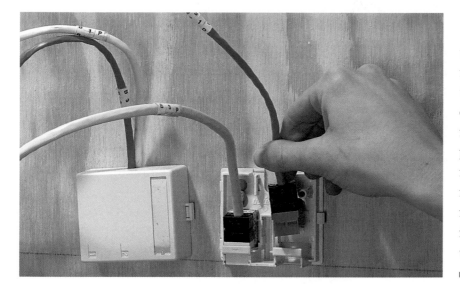

THE NETWORK HUB As discussed on page 27, the heart of your data distribution system will be an Ethernet hub or switch rated for both 10baseT (10 megabits per second) and 100baseT (100 megabits per second) networks. This network hub (right) can be attached to the panel close to the surface-mount outlet boxes.

To install the hub, use a short CAT 5e patch cable to connect one of the hub's data ports to each RJ-45 outlet. If you can find data cables in a variety of colors, use as many different colors as possible so the cables will be easier to trace. Your hub will have a power adapter that will need to be plugged into an AC outlet. (Depending on what other components are to be included on your control panel, it may make sense to attach a power strip right on the panel.) If the hub does not have enough data ports for all the computers you are connecting, you will need to either find a larger hub or follow the instructions provided with the hub to "stack" two or more hubs together.

If your network wiring includes spare outlets for future use, it is not necessary to connect those outlets to the hub at this time. As your requirements change, it will be easy to connect those extra outlets later, presuming you make careful records of your connections now. As discussed on page 62, make a list of data outlets that includes the following information for each outlet:

- The ID number of the network cable
- The room where the other end of the cable is located
- The connector number on the outlet panel or box
- The data port number on the hub connected to this outlet

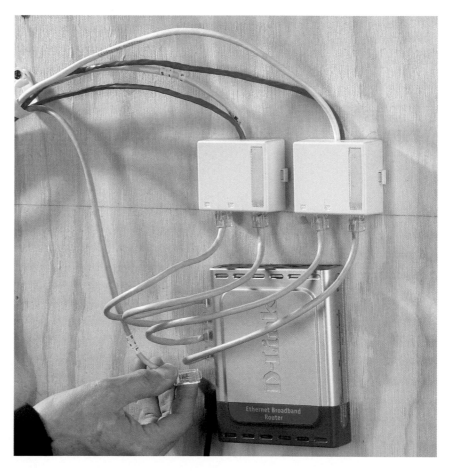

A modem and a gateway router are often best located near a computer so you can monitor the devices when troubleshooting Internet access problems.

If that data distribution hub is in another location, install the modem and the gateway router in the computer room and connect the router to a second hub in the control center.

INSTALLING AN AUDIO DISTRIBUTION SYSTEM

If audio cables are to pass through your network panel, the cables from audio sources should be securely connected to the cables to remote speakers or amplifiers. Follow these steps:

1 Fasten the terminal strips in place
Use wood screws to attach two terminal strips to the panel. The terminal strip on the left should

ADDING AN INTERNET GATEWAY
Cable, satellite, and DSL Internet services use special modems to translate high-speed data from the format used by the Internet connection to the one used on the local network. If your Internet service provider doesn't supply the modem, it will tell you exactly which make and model to use and where to buy one.

In order to connect the high-speed Internet service to more than one computer, you'll need to install a gateway router (shown above) to communicate between the Internet connection and your local network. It is generally impractical to have either the modem or the gateway router built into your network control panel.

UNDERSTANDING HUBS, SWITCHES, AND ROUTERS

Data networks use three different kinds of devices to share and exchange data.

A hub is a simple device that connects several outlets in order to share data among all of the devices connected to those outlets. In more general terms, the word *hub* is also used to describe any location or device where data signals are combined.

A data switch is a more sophisticated device that transfers each incoming data packet to a specific destination on the same network.

A router exchanges data between networks, such as between your local network and the Internet.

For a relatively simple home network, the best choice is usually a gateway router, which

combines a switch and router in a single device that connects directly to the DSL or cable modem and provides several switched data ports for your computers. If this combined unit doesn't have enough ports to meet all your needs, you have the option of connecting a simple hub or switch to one of the gateway router's local data ports.

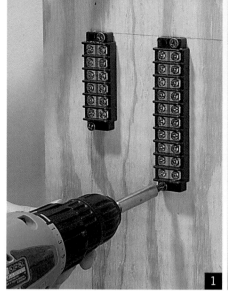

have two pairs of screw terminals for each program source. (Allow two terminal pairs for stereo, five or more pairs for surround sound.) The terminal strip on the right should have a pair of terminals for every destination.

2 Add ring lugs

Strip about ¼ inch of the insulation from the end of each wire in every cable to be attached to the network panel. With a crimping tool attach ring lugs to the ends of the wires. Avoid spade lugs, which can slip out of a terminal over time.

3 Attach the source and destination wires

Connect the wires from audio sources to terminals on the left side of the left terminal strip. Label the wires to identify the source of each cable. Connect the wires leading to speakers or amplifiers to terminals on the right side of the right terminal strip. Again, label your cables to identify the destination of each.

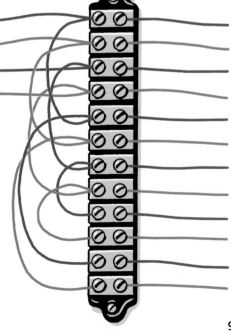

In this example, two pairs of incoming source wires are connected from one terminal block to the other. Then, by means of jumper wires, the source wires are connected to six outgoing speaker pairs. Note that no more than two ring lugs are connected to each terminal.

4 Add the cross connections

Cut a set of cross-connect cables, using the same type of audio cable that you've used for your audio wiring throughout the house. Make these pieces 2 to 3 inches longer than the distance between the two terminal strips and attach a ring lug at each end. Install a cross-connect cable from the first program source on the left terminal strip to the first destination on the right terminal strip.

5 Add jumpers

Install a jumper wire from the inside of the first destination terminal to the next destination terminal receiving the same program source. Repeat for each additional destination. No terminal should have more than two wires. Install cross-connect cables and jumper cables for each source and set of destinations.

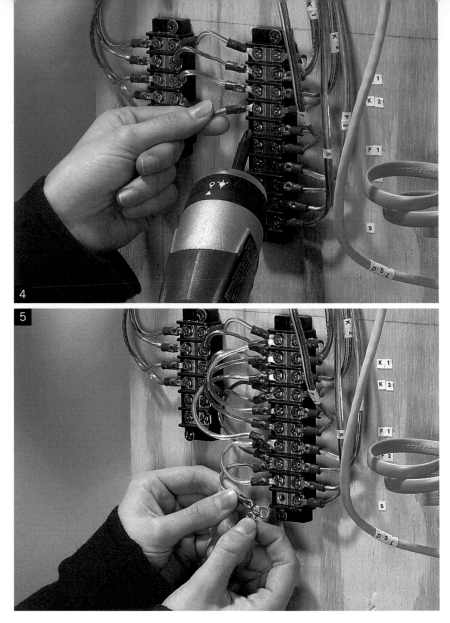

AUDIO DISTRIBUTION AS A SEPARATE SYSTEM

An audio distribution system can be part of a combined home network control center, but many audiophiles prefer to make it a separate system. Different listeners may want different CDs or different radio stations. Thus the control center for the sound system is more conveniently located someplace like the family room or the den rather than tucked away in a more remote location, where network control panels normally reside. The audio control center should include these components:

- Program sources such as CD or DVD players, AM/FM tuner, cassette deck, and turntable
- Amplifiers for speakers in the same room
- Amplifiers for speakers in other rooms
- Selectors for amplifiers, boom boxes, and stereo systems in other rooms

In an audio distribution system where the connections need to change frequently, a professional patch panel (available from audio dealers) is the best way to connect program sources to destinations. But in most home systems, the added flexibility may not be worth the extra cost. The simple selector switches built into most power amplifiers are usually sufficient for all but the most sophisticated systems.

INSTALLING A TELEPHONE DISTRIBUTION POINT TO A NETWORK PANEL

Unlike a data network, in which all computers are connected, a household telephone system can include two or more telephone lines, each distributed to various locations. For example, the main family telephone number (line 1) might have extensions in the kitchen, family room, master bedroom, home office, and den, but the line used for the fax machine (line 3) shows up only in the office. If the children have their own line (line 2), that number might have extensions in their bedrooms and in the kitchen. As the family grows and requirements change, the lines needed in each room will also likely evolve. A central distribution point makes such changes easy to accommodate.

Unless you're building a new home or doing an extensive remodel, there are usually outlets already in place for exten-

sions in some rooms. If those outlets meet your current needs, go ahead and use them. But it's still a good idea to add access to the telephone lines at the network control panel so that you can use any new network wiring to meet the changing needs of your phone system.

CONNECTING INCOMING TELEPHONE LINES TO THE CONTROL CENTER

Each telephone line comes into your house through two wires at a network interface device, which is usually mounted on an outside wall (left). The interface device includes a modular jack where you can plug in a telephone to confirm that you are receiving a dial tone. In older

A household telephone network might include three lines: one for the folks, one for the fax, and one for the kids.

homes, the phone lines may enter through protector blocks without a modular jack, but telephone company installers generally replace these blocks with a modern interface device when they add new telephone lines. In any event, either the network interface device or the protector block is the place where your telephone wiring inside the house connects to the outside lines.

The wires from every telephone outlet in your house must connect to the network interface device or protector block through one or more terminal blocks. The telephone outlets in an older house may connect in a series,

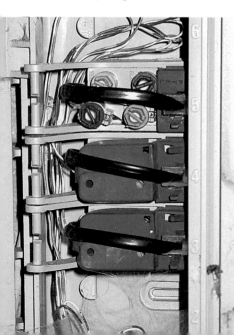

but all new outlets should connect directly to a distribution point.

Network interface devices and protector blocks were designed for use with old-fashioned four-wire telephone cables. Each telephone line has two or more color-coded screw terminals. The net effect is that homes of any age typically have a real tangle of wiring for existing phone lines and extensions. Deciphering the connections takes some experience, so you will usually do well to bring in a professional phone technician to help you work around the existing wiring.

In new construction, where no old extensions are already in place, have your technician run one or more CAT 5e cables from the network interface device to the home network control panel.

To connect the incoming phone lines to a new control panel without disrupting the existing outlets, run a length of CAT 5e cable from the old terminal block closest to the service entry directly to the control panel. If the terminal blocks are too far apart to use a single cable for more than one line, use a separate cable for each line.

Nowadays, the same cables may carry both telephone and data to the new outlets throughout the house, so it's helpful to put your new telephone distribution panel close to the data distribution panel. In a modular system (see page 110), the telephone panel is a snap-in unit that has terminals for both the incoming lines from the telephone company and the extensions to the household, along with jacks that let you connect specific lines to each room. The equivalent in a control panel you make for yourself is a component called a 66 block (see page 104).

CONNECTING A 66 BLOCK A 66 block has 50 rows of four punch-down terminals. Look for a block that is specifically rated for CAT 5e wiring. You may want to purchase an optional mounting bracket for the

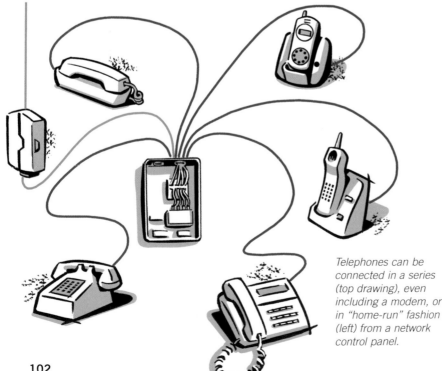

Telephones can be connected in a series (top drawing), even including a modem, or in "home-run" fashion (left) from a network control panel.

TIP AND RING

TIP

RING

The two wires that connect a telephone set are called "tip" and "ring" because they connected to the tip and ring sections of a plug in an old-fashioned telephone switchboard.

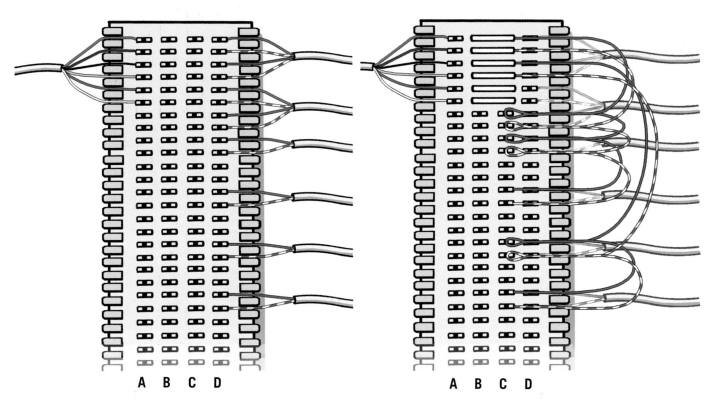

A   B   C   D   A   B   C   D

66 blocks to help hold and organize the cables.

The 66 block has four columns of terminals. Think of them as columns A, B, C, and D. You need to purchase what is called a split block, in which the terminals in columns A and B of each row are connected to each other but not to the terminals in columns C and D. The two outside columns (A and D) connect the block to incoming telephone lines and their extensions. The two inside columns (B and C) are used to cross-connect the two types of lines. (This allows incoming line 1, for example, to

be linked to four or more separate extensions.) In the illustration above, there are three incoming trunk lines linking to eight extensions.

A punch-down tool with a head specifically made for the terminals on a 66 block (below, left) is the ideal tool for telephone wiring. You simply lay the

wire over the terminal, place the tool head over the terminal, and push down. The tool has a blade on one side that will automatically trim the wire after it is pushed into place. To connect a wire without cutting it, simply reverse the tool head. If you are not making a lot of connections, you may not want to invest in

A 66 block punch-down tool head

COLOR CODE FOR CONNECTING PHONE CABLE

LINE NUMBER	TERMINAL COLOR	CAT 5E CABLE
1 (tip)	Green	Blue
1 (ring)	Red	Blue/White
2 (tip)	Black	Orange
2 (ring)	Yellow	Orange/White
3 (tip)	Green	Green
3 (ring)	Red	Green/White
4 (tip)	Black	Brown
4 (ring)	Yellow	Brown/White

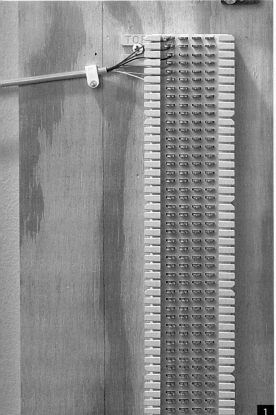

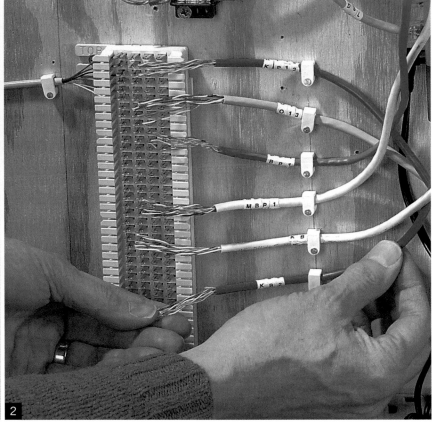

UNPLUG THE LINE

The electrical current that makes a telephone ring doesn't pose serious danger of injury, but it can give you a shock. You may want to unplug the line at the network interface before you work on your telephone system. Remember to plug the line back into the interface after the installation is finished. If there's no modular interface device on the line, don't connect the telephone lines to the protector block until the rest of the installation is complete.

this relatively pricey tool. Instead, use longnose pliers to push the wires into the terminal. Trim them off with nipper pliers.

The procedures that follow cover the wiring for three incoming lines and eight extensions. Adapt this approach to suit your particular needs.

1 Attaching the block

Install a 66 block vertically at about eye level. Fasten it in place with wood screws. Have a telephone technician extend your lines from the service entry to your network panel. He or she will likely use standard CAT 3 voice cable (see the photo

above), a six-wire cable carrying three lines to the panel. The green and red wires are line 1, connecting to rows 1 and 2; the black and yellow wires are line 2, connected to terminal rows 3 and 4. The blue and white wires are line 3, connected to rows 5 and 6.

2 Bring in the extensions

Run CAT 5e cable for your extensions. One cable can carry up to four extensions, one line for each pair of cables. In this example, only two cables carry more than one line. However, the CAT 5e cable will provide plenty of capacity for the future.

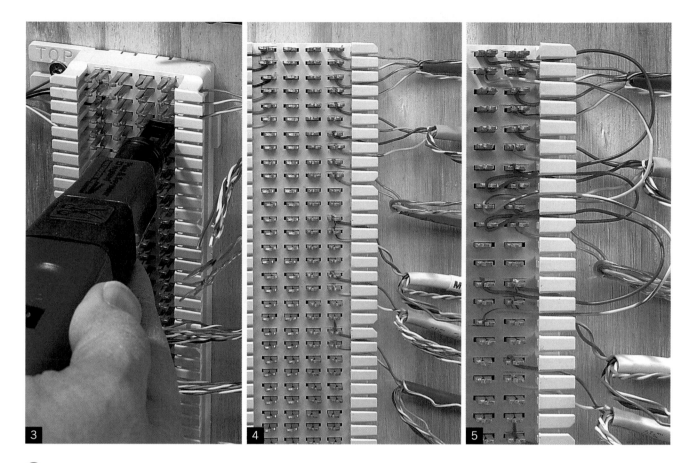

3 **Begin connecting wires**

Starting at the top right corner of the terminal block, begin connecting the extension lines. Begin with the first pair of extensions that will connect to lines 1 and 2. In this example, the topmost cable carries both line 1 and line 2 to the kitchen, so two pairs of wires are used (see illustration on page 103). Punch down and cut off the extension wires to their terminals in column D. To avoid confusion, use the blue and blue/white wires for all line 1 connections on your panel. This will make it easier to make the right connection to your RJ-11

jack at the line's destination outlet (see page 106).

4 **Tying in more lines**

The second extension cable runs to a single outlet in the home office, including line 3, a fax line, and line 1, one of the two voice lines coming into the house. Wire these extensions, as well as the four other extensions (two line 1 extensions and two line 2 extensions). Bend back unused wires; they may be useful in the future.

5 **Adding jumper wires**

Make jumper wires from CAT 5e cable. Cut off a foot or two of

cable and use strippers and pliers to pull the twisted wire pairs out of the jacket. Punch down one end of the solid blue wire in the column C terminal for line 1, trimming the wire end in the process. Reverse the punch-down tool head so it pushes the wire into the terminal but doesn't cut it. Lay the wire in the grooves along the side of the 66 block. Route the blue wire to the column C terminal for the first extension that will connect to line 2—in this case terminal 7 of column C. Punch it in. Use the same jumper wire to connect the tip wires (solid blue) of the other line 1 extensions.

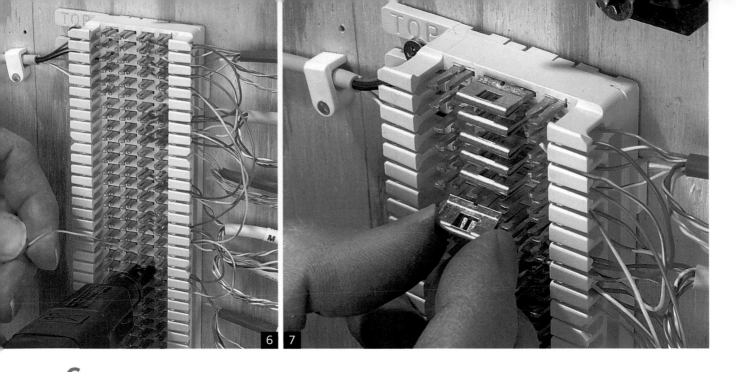

6 Completing the jumpers
Add orange and orange/white jumpers to link the incoming line 2 with its extensions. Remember to punch down the wire but not cut it off at terminals where the wire jumps. Then reverse the head to cut the first and last connection.

7 Add bridging clips
Because the terminals in columns A and B are connected to each other but not to those in C and D, you'll need to link columns B and C to connect all the terminals in a row. Use bridging clips to extend each incoming line across the row. The clips push into place. In this example, bridging clips connect rows 1 through 6.

CONNECTING TO TELEPHONE JACKS

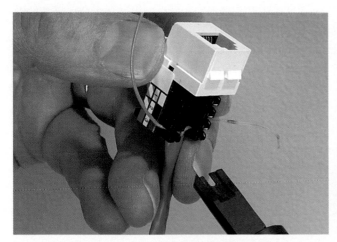

To connect one telephone extension to an RJ-11 jack, unravel the appropriately colored wired pair and punch them into place (in this case the blue pair extension of line 1). Line 1 wires always connect to pins 3 and 4 of the RJ-11 connector, regardless of the colors on the jack.

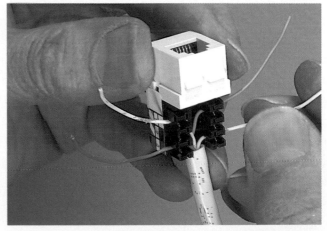

To connect two lines to a single jack, connect two of the twisted pairs in a CAT 5e cable from the 66 block, following the color codes on the jack. In this example, the blue–blue/white pair carries line 1, and the green–green/white pair carries line 3.

DISTRIBUTING VIDEO IN A NETWORK

A household video distribution system can perform these functions:

- Distribute cable or satellite programs to TV sets and FM radios in various rooms
- Carry programs from a videotape or DVD player throughout the house
- Add programs from a rooftop antenna to the programs from cable or satellite
- Send and receive Internet data through a cable modem

Each of these functions uses a different method to connect to the cable, so it's important to plan your system carefully. If the signal processors connected to the cable are arranged in the wrong order, the system may not work properly.

For any system that does more than just receive TV and FM programs and Internet service from a cable TV or satellite service and distribute it throughout the house, the best choice is a modular system. Leviton's Structured Home Entertainment Package and Pass & Seymour's Modular Home Network Center both include a modulator to add

signals from local sources. These systems include compact and easy-to-install video modules that are designed to work together well. Each of these products includes detailed installation instructions.

The illustration below shows a video network with just about every type of service such a system could support. Your own network might not include this many options, but the illustration should make clear how your components should interrelate.

COMBINING SIGNALS FROM MORE THAN ONE SOURCE A video distribution network cable carries many program channels through the same cable, each operating at a different set of radio frequencies. In order to add a program to the cable, a device called a modulator is needed to assign that program to an

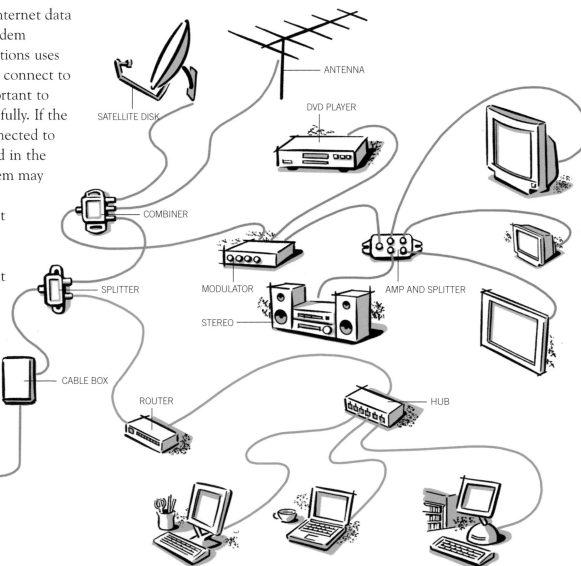

ANTENNA

SATELLITE DISK

DVD PLAYER

COMBINER

SPLITTER

MODULATOR

STEREO

AMP AND SPLITTER

CABLE BOX

ROUTER

HUB

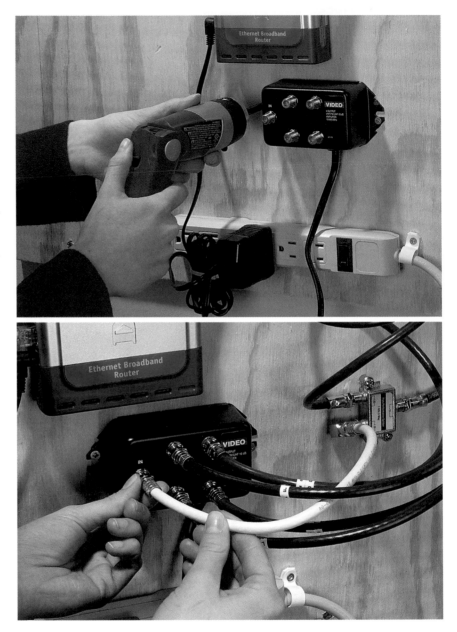

The amp and splitter mount to the board with wood screws (right). A suitable video setup for a "homebrew" network panel (below) includes a splitter that routes a video cable to a cable modem with a jumper cable to an amplifier that sends four cables to various points in the house.

unused channel. Thus a program from a VCR or DVD must pass through the modulator before it is added to the distribution signal.

To combine radio signals from the cable TV service, a modulator, and an antenna, use a module that mixes incoming signals into a single output signal. Such combiner modules are available as stand-alone units or as part of a device that takes multiple incoming signals and routes them to various destinations.

A SIMPLE WAY TO BOOST AND DISTRIBUTE VIDEO The splitter-and-amplifier combination shown on the network panel at right will give four video outlets a strong, clear signal while splitting off a cable for an Internet connection through a cable modem.

The amplifier is necessary because video signals are weakened every time they pass through a splitter. TV receivers are sensitive enough to handle signals from weak over-the-air stations, so a two- or three-way split doesn't usually cause a problem. But when the signal

must go to four or more destinations, amplification is needed to provide enough signal strength. Signal amplifiers can also be used without the splitter, if you're not using the cable for your Internet connection.

Most video amplifiers operate in only one direction, from

source to destination. However, data for an Internet connection must be able to move in two directions, so it's important to route the signal to your cable modem around, not through, the amplifier. That's the job of the splitter. Likewise, video players set up to broadcast to other parts of the house should connect to a splitter and bypass the amplifier. Although they do not use a two-way signal, they are sending a signal in a direction opposite to that of the incoming cable signal.

CONNECTING A CABLE MODEM

For best performance, the cable modem should connect to the incoming service on a separate RG6/U cable that bypasses the amplifiers needed to boost and distribute the video signals to TV sets and FM radios in other parts of the house (see illustration below).

Starting at the service entry, where the line from your cable television provider comes into the house, run a cable to a splitter. One output from this splitter can connect directly to the cable modem. The other splitter output should connect to the video distribution system.

The best location for the modem is usually next to a computer and the gateway router. The cable company's technician will install and test the cable modem and and also make sure that you've got a good connection from the service entry to the computer room.

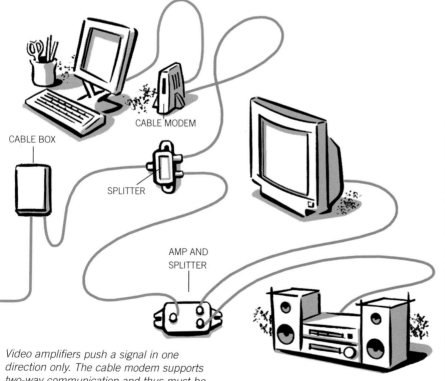

CABLE MODEM

CABLE BOX

SPLITTER

AMP AND
SPLITTER

Video amplifiers push a signal in one direction only. The cable modem supports two-way communication and thus must be wired to bypass the amp, usually by means of a splitter.

KEEPING IT SIMPLE WITH YOUR VIDEO

Setting up a complex video distribution system can be both confusing and expensive, because of the need for splitters, combiners, amplifiers, and the like. Before embarking on such a mission, consider the alternatives:

Most cable TV companies will install the inside wiring and outlets for their service in one or more rooms when they connect the house to the cable. See what kind of help your company offers. If there's going to be an outlet in each room with a TV set and you don't plan to add signals from an antenna or a DVD player, you may already have adequate arrangements for all the video wiring you will need. If the cable installers will do the work for you, by all means, take advantage of that service.

An alternative to creating a distribution system that carries movies and other recorded programs from a central location is to install an inexpensive DVD or videotape player next to each TV set. You don't need to spend a lot for high-quality recording machines if they're going to be used only to play prerecorded programs.

adding an off-the-shelf network control panel

Modular home network panels, including Leviton's Structured Media Centers and Pass & Seymour's Home Network Center, are designed to provide all of a household's network services within a single enclosure. These panels are typically 14½ inches wide so that they can fit into the standard 16-inch space between studs. Modular network panels have snap-in, prewired modules that connect telephone, data, video, and audio wiring. They offer a quick and relatively easy way to configure network wiring.

Such preconfigured network control panels are considerably more expensive than panels assembled from individual parts, but they offer an attractive alternative for homeowners seeking ease of installation and consistent appearance.

INSTALLING A MODULAR NETWORK PANEL

Before mounting a panel on a finished wall, decide whether the front of the panel will be flush with the wall or the entire panel mounted on the surface. If the cables come into the room inside the wall, a flush-mount panel is the better choice; but if the cables come through an exposed hole in the ceiling or via a PVC conduit (see page 20), there's no reason to cut into the wall.

To install a modular panel, begin by selecting the enclosure and modules that meet the specific needs of your network. Available models include distribution modules for voice and data, modules for audio, and splitters for video. Each module mounts on the enclosure with push-in pins (left).

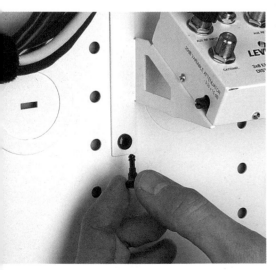

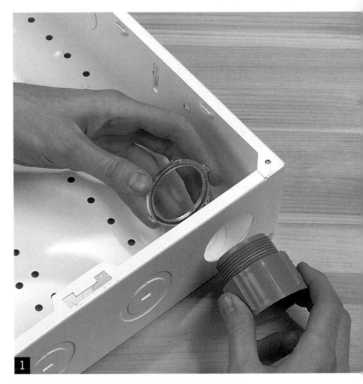

1 Prepare the enclosure

Remove the knock-out access holes at the top and bottom of the panel. The cables from the network outlets will pass through the holes in the top; AC power wiring will enter through the bottom. Insert protective grommets into all of the access holes. These keep your cables from being damaged as they are pulled into the panel.

2 Cut the opening and insert the panel

If you decide on flush mounting, use an electronic stud finder to locate the studs inside the wall. Choose the exact position where you want to place the control panel. The top of the enclosure should be slightly higher than eye level, with enough space above the panel for network cables and enough space below for AC power. Measure and cut a hole between the studs about ¾ inch longer than the panel. If you are dealing with existing walls, it's easiest to run cable before installing the box; feed the cables through the protective grommets as you insert the panel. (If you have open framing, you may want to install the panel first. Simply choose your location and fasten the panel between two studs.)

3 Fasten the enclosure in place

Use general-purpose screws to attach both sides of the panel to the studs through the mounting holes. If there is space between one side of the enclosure and the stud, tap in a couple of pieces of wood shim before fastening.

4 Install the AC power module

Because many modules have transformers that must be plugged into a 120-volt AC power source, an AC module must be installed. Check with your local building department about code and inspection requirements for extending a circuit. Unless you have experience installing AC wiring, hire a qualified electrician to extend a circuit to the panel location. Before making the final connection to the AC module, **shut off power to the circuit and test for power.** Follow the manufacturer's instructions for connecting the module.

SURFACE-MOUNT PANELS

To surface-mount a panel, cut a piece of 3/8- to 3/4-inch plywood to the height of the panel and about 19 inches wide. Be sure to fasten mounting screws into the framing, not just into the wall material. Use a stud finder to locate the studs, and then use general-purpose screws that are at least twice as long as the combined thickness of the wall material and the plywood. Attach the panel to the plywood through the mounting holes, piercing dimples on the back of the enclosure. Avoid using the grid of holes provided for attaching the modules.

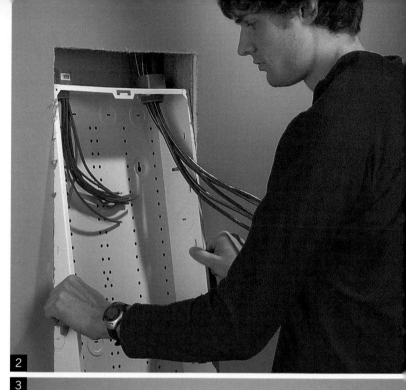

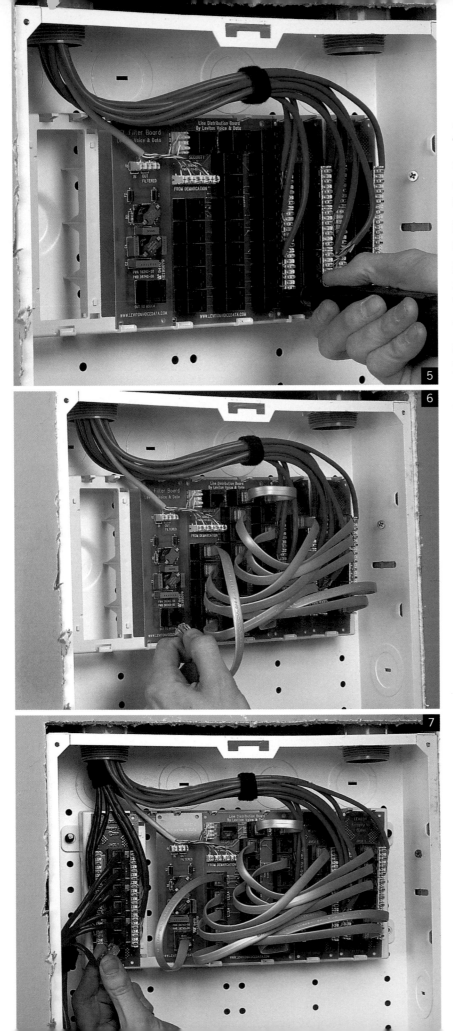

5 Install the voice module

The telephone and data modules use color-coded punch-down terminals to connect the CAT 5e cables. Use either the plastic tool supplied with the modules or a spring-mounted punch-down tool to attach the individual wires to the terminals. To connect the telephone wiring, run a CAT 5e cable (the gray cable shown) from the telephone company's service entry (the "demarcation point") and connect the individual wire pairs to the "From Demarcation" terminal strip on the telephone line distribution module (TLDM). Be sure the wiring follows the color code supplied with the module.

6 Add the patch cords

Leviton and other suppliers offer several types of modules for connecting extension telephone lines from outlets throughout the house to the incoming trunk lines. The in-house CAT 5e wiring connects to these modules through punch-down terminal strips. To connect telephone lines to the in-house modules, use the patch cables that are supplied with the modules.

7 Install the data module

Snap the data module into place and connect the CAT 5e cables (in this example, the purple cables) that run to the data wall jacks throughout the house.

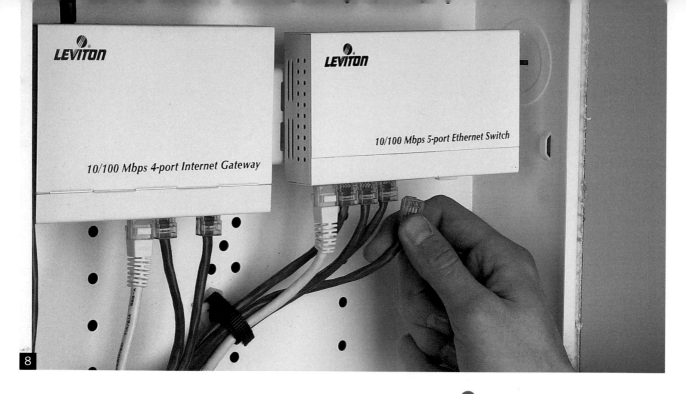

Attach the patch cords (in this case, red) that will connect the module to the Internet gateway and the Ethernet switch.

8 Install and connect the Internet gateway and Ethernet switch

Install the Internet gateway and the Ethernet switch and then attach the patch cords to link the jacks of the data module to the data ports on the router and hub. Also hook up the incoming DSL circuit from the modem to the Internet gateway. Leviton offers a hub as part of its Structured Cabling product line, but it's also possible to use a less costly 10/100 Mbps hub from another manufacturer, such as D-Link, Linksys, Belkin, or Netgear.

9 Add the video module

The video modules use F connectors (in this case, Leviton's own brand) to connect video cables from the antenna or cable TV service entry to distribution cables inside the house through splitters and combiners. Follow the instructions supplied with each module.

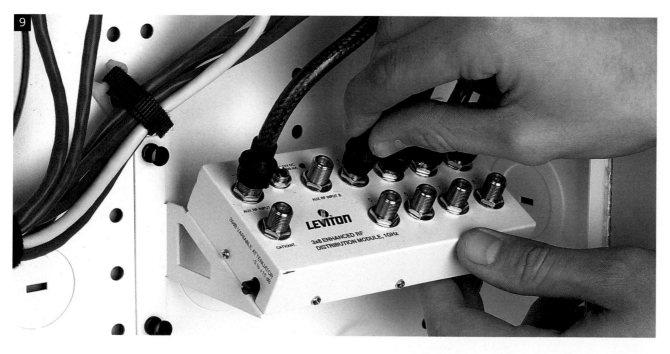

Each of the many devices that can tie into your network will require different steps to make the connection. Some will involve nothing more than configuration software; others will require that you plug them in.

making the connections

ONCE THE WIRING FOR YOUR NETWORK IS COMPLETE and all the cables have been hooked up through the network panel, the final step is to actually connect the various devices you're going to use—the computers, telephones, televisions, and so forth. This chapter explains how to make these connections and how to configure your computers and other devices to communicate with the outside world. ■ *Connecting a telephone to a wall jack is easy enough, but some of the other connections are a bit more complicated. Linking a computer to the Internet requires not only the proper jack and expansion card in your machine, but also software that configures the computer to the specifications of your Internet service provider. Even tying into your own data network or hooking up a television to the cable outlet through a set-top box can pose challenges.* ■ *Some homeowners find that this stage of the project proves every bit as demanding as the installation of the network. All the cable hookups and settings have to be exactly right or the connection will probably fail. To minimize confusion, work on connecting only one device at a time and confirm that it's working just right before moving on.*

connecting the data network

Every computer, printer, scanner, game box or other device connected to your data network has to have a wired or wireless link to the hub that ties them together. The hub also connects your machines to the Internet via a router. For such a system to work, each computer requires an interface that allows it to exchange data with the network. This interface can come in a variety of forms:

■ A built-in interface that is part of the computer
■ An expansion card that fits inside the computer's processor unit
■ An external adapter that connects to the computer through a USB cable
■ A plug-in adapter that fits the PC card socket in a laptop computer

On a laptop computer, the jack for a built-in network outlet

Inexpensive network adapters (below) for Windows-based computers fit into the expansion slots inside the processor unit. Most computers made since about 1999 use PCI sockets for expansion cards; older computers have ISA sockets. If you have a wireless hub, you can link a laptop to it with a PCM-CIA network card (right).

is usually on the back or the side of the case. If there is no built-in data jack, use a credit-card-sized adapter that fits into the PC card slot on the side of the computer.

On a desktop computer, the network connector is almost always an RJ-45 jack at the back of the housing. Look for this jack on the same panel that has connectors for the mouse, keyboard, monitor, and printer.

Apple Macintosh computers and many machines that use Microsoft Windows have such built-in network adapters. If there's an RJ-45 Ethernet jack on the computer's rear panel, a network adapter is already in place. If there isn't a built-in network outlet, install a network interface card in one of the expansion slots.

If there isn't a network adapter, it's usually not difficult to add one in one of the computer's expansion slots. Look for an adapter that supports both the 10baseT (10 Mbps) and 100baseT (100 Mbps) standards at a computer store or office supply store.

ADDING AN EXPANSION CARD
Installing an expansion card in a desktop computer is a straightforward procedure.

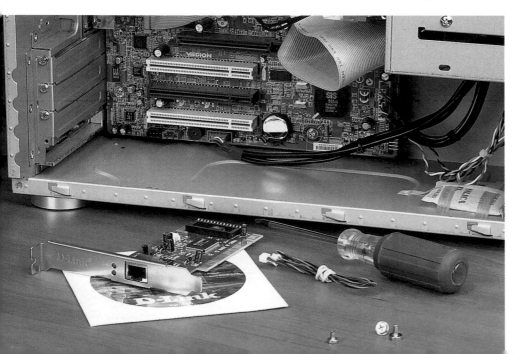

1 Open the computer

Turn the computer off and disconnect the AC power cable. Open or remove the cover to the computer's processor unit. Use a blast of compressed air or a small vacuum cleaner to remove any dust that has accumulated inside the case. Look for an unused expansion socket near the back of the motherboard.

2 Slide the card into the socket

Remove the metal cover insert next to the socket that you plan to use. Slide the network adapter card into the socket, making certain that the card is firmly seated.

3 Secure the adapter card

Use the screw that held the cover insert to secure the adapter card to the frame. Replace the cover and connect the AC power cord.

4 Install the software

Replace the cover and turn on the computer. The operating system should automatically detect the presence of the new network adapter. Follow the on-screen instructions for installing the software that controls the adapter.

CONNECTING TO A MODEM

The data network usually connects to the Internet through either a DSL modem, a cable modem, or a modem that connects to a dial-up telephone line. The connection will be one of following:

■ A cable modem connected to a cable TV wall outlet with an RG6/U video cable

■ A DSL modem linked to a data outlet with a CAT 5e cable

■ A telephone modem connected to a telephone line jack

If your Internet service provider includes a special crossover cable with the cable or DSL modem, use it to connect the modem to the router. However, a crossover cable uses pin assignments slightly different from standard CAT 5e connections and cannot be used interchangeably with a patch cord.

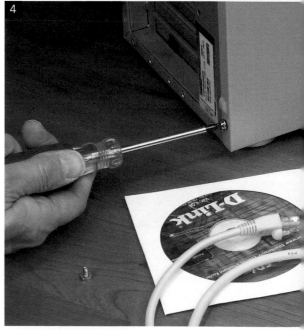

CONNECTING COMPUTERS TO THE NETWORK

Before making connections to your computers, disconnect AC power and turn off the hub or router, the cable or DSL modem, and the computer that's located closest to the router. This will ensure that the network doesn't try to automatically configure itself before all the components are connected. Use preassembled CAT 5e cables to connect each computer's RJ-45 connector to a hub or a wall outlet. After all the cables are in place, turn on the AC power on each device in the network.

If your data network has its network panel in a different location from the router and the DSL or cable modem (below), connect the uplink port on the hub in the network panel to one of the data ports on the router. If the network hub and the control panel are in the same room, run a CAT 5e cable from the router or hub directly to the outlet connected to each remote computer.

To set up the network, configure the connections in this order:

- The first computer should exchange data with the router.
- The router should exchange data with the Internet.
- The first computer should exchange data with the Internet.
- The remaining computers should exchange data with the Internet and with other computers on the network.

Begin the process by setting up the computer closest to the router to send commands to the router. Then use that computer to configure the router to connect to the Internet. As data moves through the network, the lights on the front of the router and the modem should flash.

Every computer and local network connected to the Internet has a unique address made up of four sets of numbers (198.163.100.24, for example). Your network will also use several other addresses to make the connection. Your Internet service provider (ISP) will supply the necessary information, including the following:

- The IP (Internet Protocol) address, if any, permanently assigned to your account
- A "subnet mask" address
- The Network Gateway address

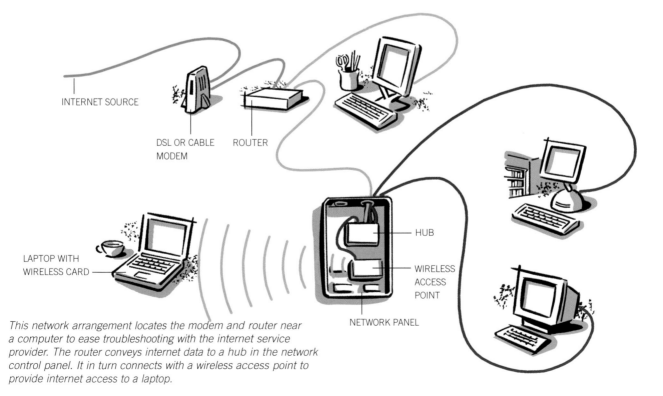

INTERNET SOURCE

DSL OR CABLE MODEM

ROUTER

HUB

WIRELESS ACCESS POINT

LAPTOP WITH WIRELESS CARD

NETWORK PANEL

This network arrangement locates the modem and router near a computer to ease troubleshooting with the internet service provider. The router conveys internet data to a hub in the network control panel. It in turn connects with a wireless access point to provide internet access to a laptop.

■ Two or more DNS (Domain Name Server) addresses
■ A telephone number for live technical support

Your ISP should also provide addresses and passwords for the e-mail mailboxes attached to your account. This information isn't necessary for setting up the network connection, but you will need it later.

Follow the instructions in the computer's online help resource to configure the network connection. You'll also need the printed manual or quick-start guide supplied with the router to set up that part of your system.

Some Internet service providers, including America Online (AOL), Microsoft Network (MSN), and Yahoo!, supply software for new accounts on CD-ROMs. Other service providers may offer printed configuration instructions. In either case, run the setup program from the disc, or follow the printed instructions, only after you've set the first computer to communicate with the router.

CONNECTING THROUGH A TELEPHONE LINE

If a high-speed DSL or cable connection to the Internet is not available, your home network will need to connect through a telephone line instead. In this approach, one of the network computers uses a modem to place a telephone call to your ISP. The computer then shares that connection with the other machines on your network.

To set up a phone line connection in Windows, run the Network Setup Wizard on the computer with the modem. Choose the option "This computer connects directly to the Internet."

For a Mac running OS X, go to the Apple menu and choose *System Preferences*. From the View menu, choose *Network*. Choose *Internal Modem* from the Show pop-up menu. If your computer does not have a built-in modem, select your external modem. Then type in the information provided by your ISP.

All of the remaining computers and other network devices will connect to a dial-up network through the network hub in exactly the same way they connect to a high-speed link.

MAKING WIRELESS NETWORK CONNECTIONS

If any of the computers in your home network will connect to the network through wireless links, the network should include a wireless access point or base station that follows

Once you've equipped your laptop with a PCMCIA network card (see page 116), you'll need to add a wireless access point to your network before you can enjoy the ease of wireless communication.

Wi-Fi standards. The access point can either be part of the same router that connects to other computers through cables or be a separate unit connected by a cable to one of the Ethernet ports on the router.

Each computer that uses a wireless link will need a wireless network adapter. For desktop computers, choose a wireless adapter that fits an internal expansion slot or one that uses the computer's USB ports. Many laptop computers and other portable devices now have built-in Wi-Fi capability; if yours does not, you can use an adapter that fits into the PCMCIA socket on the side of the computer.

thing is set correctly, the Web pages will appear.

If you can't connect to the Internet, confirm that all the settings are correct. In particular, make sure that the DHCP setting for your network is right and that the router's connection to the WAN (the ISP's Wide Area Network) is set to the correct option. The router either will use a set IP address or will automatically obtain the address from the ISP. If this doesn't work, you'll need technical support from your ISP.

CONFIGURING WINDOWS

In Microsoft Windows XP, follow these steps to set up the network. (The setup is similar in older versions of Windows, but the text on individual screens may vary slightly.)

From the Start menu, choose *Settings > Control Panel > Network Setup Wizard.* Step through the Wizard screens until you see the "Select a connection method" page. Choose the "This computer connects through a residential gateway" option and click on the Next button.

Next, provide a description and a name for the computer. The network will use this information to identify the computer,

Remember to change the default password on the wireless access point; also turn on the wireless security features. This will make it more difficult for intruders to steal Internet access or read your personal files.

CONFIGURING THE ROUTER

Use the computer closest to the router to set up its connection to the network. You'll need to follow the detailed configuration instructions supplied by the router's manufacturer. These will generally be in the user's manual or in a separate quick-start guide. Use the IP, subnet, gateway, and DNS addresses supplied by your Internet service provider.

One of the settings in the router configuration screen will ask whether DHCP (Dynamic Host Configuration Protocol) should be active (or enabled) on the local network. DHCP is a set of rules that allow the router to automatically assign addresses to each computer connected to it. You will want to activate DHCP in the router that connects to the Internet.

If your network includes additional router/hubs, however, turn off DHCP on those devices. The router connected to the Internet access device should provide DHCP for the whole network.

After configuring the router and the first computer, confirm that the Internet connection is working properly. Open a Web browser and try to view a couple of Web sites. If every-

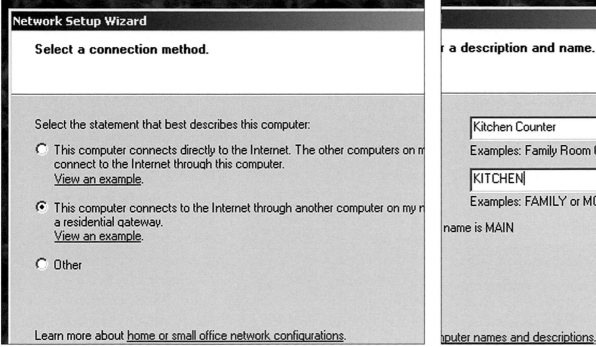

Network Setup Wizard

Select a connection method.

Select the statement that best describes this computer:

○ This computer connects directly to the Internet. The other computers on m connect to the Internet through this computer.
 <u>View an example.</u>

◉ This computer connects to the Internet through another computer on my r a residential gateway.
 <u>View an example.</u>

○ Other

Learn more about <u>home or small office network configurations</u>.

r a description and name.

Kitchen Counter

Examples: Family Room Computer or Monica's Co

KITCHEN|

Examples: FAMILY or MONICA

name is MAIN

nputer names and descriptions.

Microsoft Windows XP comes with Network Setup Wizard, which can be used to configure Internet and network connections. This program presents step-by-step options (above) for configuring the various comput-ers on your network, asking you to identify each one (above right). You'll need to run the Network Setup Wizard on all of your computers before the configuration of your network is complete.

so each computer should have a different name. Click the Next button to move to the next screen.

Don't change the MSHOME setting in the Workgroup name field. Click the Next button. (The Workgroup name must be exactly the same for all the computers on your network.)

Choose the "Turn on file and printer sharing" option and click the Next button. Continue through the remaining Wizard screens until the "You're almost done" screen appears. Choose the "Create a Network Setup Disk" option. This setup disk will make it faster and easier to configure the other computers.

Click the Next button on each remaining screen and follow the instructions on the screen to complete the installation Wizard.

FILE SHARING FOR WINDOWS To set up file sharing among the Windows computers on your network, follow these steps:

Open the "My Computer" window from the Windows desktop. If you want to share all the files on a hard drive, select the icon for that drive and choose "Sharing and Security" from the File menu. The Local Disk Properties dialog box will open.

To share only selected folders on a drive, open the drive in My Computer and select the folders you want to share. Choose

Configuring a Mac

To set up a Macintosh running OS X to run on the network, open the Apple menu and select *System Preferences.* In the *System Preferences* window, select the *Network* icon. In the *Network Preferences* window, set these options:

■ Location: Automatic
■ Show: Built-in Ethernet
■ Configure: Using DHCP (this instructs the computer to accept address information from the network router)
■ Domain Name Servers: Enter the DNS addresses supplied by your ISP.

Click on the Apply Now button to save your settings, and quit the *System Preferences* program.

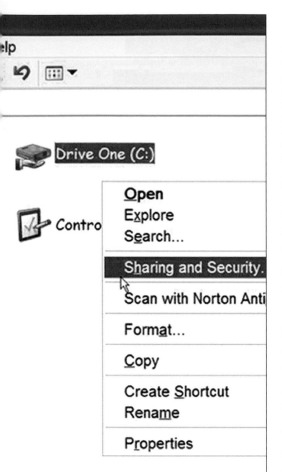

When file sharing is available, the Windows Explorer window shows a hand "serving" the icon that is accessible to other computers on the network. Windows calls these drives and folders "shares."

"Sharing and Security" from the File menu. Choose the *Sharing* tab at the top of the window and turn on the "Share this folder on the network" option. Click the OK button to save the change.

Repeat these steps for each additional drive to be shared with the network. Click on the "My Network Neighborhood" icon in the Windows desktop. The window (left) will appear, with an icon for every drive on each network computer. Click on an icon to open a shared drive.

CONNECT REMAINING COMPUTERS

Once the first computer is Internet ready, use the Network Setup Disk you made on this first machine to set up each additional Windows computer. Use the "Configuring a Mac" procedure (see page 121) to set up your Macintosh computers. All of the computers should have access to the Internet by the time your network is up and running.

With Macs, to share files and folders, turn on the file-sharing feature under the Control Panels menu on each machine. In Windows, select a drive or folder to share and click the right mouse button. Then choose the "Sharing and Security" option from the pop-up menu.

CONNECTING TELEPHONES

Use modular telephone cables with RJ-11 plugs at both ends to connect telephone sets to wall outlets or surface-mount outlet boxes. To connect a fax machine, modem, or some other device with more than one RJ-11 jack, use the jack labeled "Line." Consult the instructions provided with these devices for information on using the other jacks.

Even if a telephone outlet is wired to carry two or three separate lines, a single-line telephone set will use line 1—the one connected to pins 3 and 4 inside the wall outlet. To connect a telephone to a different line, use a special two- or three-line adapter.

If your data network uses DSL service for access to the Internet, remember to add a DSL filter to each telephone set or other device that uses the same line as the DSL modem. Plug the filter into the telephone set or the wall outlet, and plug the data cable into the filter. For telephones that use wall-mount brackets, replace the original bracket with one that has a built-in filter.

connecting video & audio

Video connections can be complicated because cable and satellite TV services provide set-top boxes that add more channels than an unaided television set can receive over the air. With the addition of a VCR, a DVD player, a game console, or a recording system such as TiVo, the result can be a confusing mass of cables. Every combination requires a different arrangement of cables and switches.

The solution is to carefully study the instructions supplied with each unit and work out a logical sequence of inputs and outputs. Some DVD players, game consoles, and set-top cable boxes have built-in switches that can select an input signal, but others may require a separate switch box.

The connection from the household cable TV distribution wall outlet connected to the set-top box is straightforward: Run an RG6/U cable from the wall outlet to the box. Both the outlet and the box have F-type sockets, so the F connectors on the cable make the job simple.

Home audio distribution can be either high-level program signals that plug into an amplifier, tabletop radio, or compact stereo, or speaker-level signals that connect either directly to remote speakers or indirectly through a volume control. If the speakers are not built into the walls, use 12- or 14-gauge speaker wire to connect from the wall outlets to the connectors on the back of the speakers.

For high-level signals, use an audio cable with RCA plugs at one end to fit the wall outlet, and connectors on the other end to mate with the Line input on the amplifier or radio.

This video and audio setup includes a television, a DVD player, a video cassette player, and surround sound.

glossary

10baseT An Ethernet standard for distributing data through twisted pair wiring at up to 10 megabits per second (mbps).

100baseT An Ethernet standard for distributing data through twisted pair wiring at up to 100 megabits per second (mbps).

110 BLOCK A type of compact terminal block that uses metal teeth to hold each wire in place.

110 TOOL A tool that forces wires into the space between the teeth in a 110 block terminal.

66 BLOCK A type of terminal block for twisted pair cables that uses metal teeth to hold each wire.

66 TOOL A tool that forces wires into the space between the teeth in a 66 block terminal.

ACCESS POINT A device that exchanges data signals between a wireless network and a wired LAN.

ADSL Asymmetric Digital Subscriber Line. DSL service in which the subscriber sends and receives data at different speeds. For example, an ADSL connection might receive data at about 1.5 Mbps, but it can transmit data at a maximum of only 128 kbps.

AMPLIFIER A device that boosts the strength of a signal.

BROADBAND A network connection or circuit that can transfer data at high speed.

CABLE MODEM A service offered by cable TV companies that moves a high-speed Internet connection through the same cable used to distribute TV programs. Also, the modem used to convert data between a cable TV system and an Ethernet network.

CAT 5E The Category of Performance specification for cable that can carry data at speeds up to 100 MHz. CAT 5e cable contains four color-coded twisted pairs of wires.

CATV Community Antenna Television. An old name for cable TV service.

CENTRAL OFFICE The building that contains the telephone company's switching equipment.

CENTRAL PROCESSOR The box that contains a computer's internal circuits. The keyboard, mouse, monitor and other devices are all connected to the central processor through cables (or they can be wireless—as with Mac Bluetooth).

CLIENT A computer or other device on a network that uses files or other resources that are provided by another device (called a server) on the same network.

COAXIAL CABLE Also called "coax." A form of wiring with one or more central wires separated by insulation from a surrounding shield. Coax can carry signals with very high bandwidth, such as video or cable TV.

CONTROL PANEL A central gathering point for receiving and distributing data, telephone, and video signals.

CUSTOMER PREMISES The telephone company's term for a location, such as a house, where they provide telephone service.

DEMARCATION The location that divides the telephone company's wiring from the house wiring. The telephone company is responsible for maintaining everything outside the demarcation point; the homeowner must maintain everything inside the demarcation point. The service entry is on the telephone company's side of the demarcation point.

DSL Digital Subscriber Link. A service offered by many telephone companies that moves high-speed data through the same copper wires used for a standard telephone line.

DSL FILTER A device that removes the noise produced by a DSL connection from the other equipment connected to the same telephone line.

DSL MODEM A modem that converts data between a DSL telephone line and an Ethernet network.

DVD Digital Video Disc, or Digital Versatile Disc. A digital storage medium that can hold up to 17 gigabytes of data. DVDs are used to carry several hours of high-quality audio or video.

ETHERNET The specification for the type of data network distribution used in many local area networks.

EXPANSION CARD A circuit board that plugs into a computer's motherboard. Video controllers, network adapters and other add-in services use expansion boards.

EXTENSION A telephone line inside a house or other building.

F CONNECTOR The connector type commonly used with coaxial cable for video and RF services.

HOME RUN WIRING A wiring system in which the cables from every outlet connect directly to a central control panel. Compare with point-to-point wiring.

HUB A device that exchanges data between two or more computers on the same network.

INTERNET The worldwide "network of networks" that allows a computer to share information with any other connected computer.

INTERNET SERVICE PROVIDER (ISP) A business that sells access to the Internet.

JACK A low-voltage receptacle or socket mounted on a panel or a wall.

JUMPER CABLE A relatively short cable with connectors on both ends.

KBPS One thousand bits per second. A unit of measure for data transmission speed.

LAN A Local Area Network. A network that connects computers within a small area, such as a single building. A home computer network is a LAN.

MBPS One million bits per second. A unit of measure for data transmission speed. 1 Mbps equals 1,000 Kbps.

MODEM A device that converts computer data to signals that can move through distribution media such as a telephone line or a cable TV system. When used without a modifier, such as "DSL modem" or "cable modem," a modem is usually a device that converts data to audio signals that can move through a voice-quality telephone line. Short for MODulator/DEModulator.

MODULATOR A device that converts a video signal to a specific TV channel, so the signal can be distributed through a cable TV system and viewed on any television set connected to the system.

MOTHERBOARD The large circuit board inside a computer's processing unit that contains the main components.

MULTIPLAYER GAMES Computer games in which two or more players compete against each other and each player is using his or her own game console or computer.

NETWORK INTERFACE A connection point that sends and receives data to and from a computer.

OUTSIDE PLANT The telephone company's term for the wiring between the central office and the customer premises. Outside plant ends at the service entry.

PATCH CORD A short cable with a connector at each end that connects a source to a destination on a patch panel, or a network adapter to a wall outlet.

PATCH PANEL A set of outlets or receptacles for data, telephone lines, audio or video that are connected to individual signal sources or destinations. A patch panel allows easy changes to a network by connecting short cables from a source outlet to a destination outlet.

PCMCIA SOCKET A receptacle found in laptop computers that accepts credit-card-sized PC card adapters. PC cards can contain modems, network interfaces, data storage, or other services.

POINT-TO-POINT WIRING A wiring system in which cables connect directly from a source to a destination, without going through a central control panel. Compare with home run wiring.

PORT An access point where a computer or other device connects to a network.

POTS Plain Old Telephone Service. A POTS line provides dial tone and access to the public telephone network but no special services, such as DSL.

PVR Personal Video Recorder. A device, such as TiVo, that uses a hard drive to record and play back television programs and other video images.

RCA PLUG A type of connector used for unbalanced high-level audio signals.

RG6/U The type designation for low-loss dual-shield coaxial cable used to distribute video signals within a building.

RJ-11 The standard plug and outlet used to connect telephone sets and other devices to one or more telephone lines.

RJ-45 The standard plug and outlet used to connect computers, hubs, switches and other devices in a network. RJ-45 connectors are commonly used in CAT 5e jumper cables and patch cords.

ROUTER A device that exchanges data between two networks, such as a home network and the Internet.

SERVER A computer or other device on a network that supplies files or other resources to another device (called a client) on the same network.

SERVICE ENTRY The terminal block where telephone or cable TV wiring from the pole or underground connects to wiring from inside the house.

SPLITTER A device that converts signals from one input to two or more outputs.

STRUCTURED WIRING A system for distribution of data, telephone and video through a house, in which every wall outlet includes all three types of signal connected from a central control panel.

SWITCH In a data network, a device that automatically selects circuits between computers connected to the network.

TERMINAL BLOCK A device that connects wires.

TRUNK A telephone line that connects a building to the telephone company's central office. Each trunk line carries a unique telephone number. A single trunk may be connected to one or more extensions.

TWISTED PAIR A type of cable that contains one or more set of two wires that are twisted around each other in order to reduce interference. CAT 5e cable contains four twisted pairs.

USB Universal Serial Bus. A type of computer port that can connect external devices, including digital cameras, scanners and wired or wireless network interfaces to a desktop or laptop computer.

VCR Video Cassette Recorder. A device that records and plays analog videotape recordings.

WAN Wide Area Network. A network that uses telephone lines or other media to connect computers in more than one physical location. Internet service providers use WANs to connect their subscribers to the Internet.

WI-FI The specification for wireless Ethernet networks. Short for "Wireless Fidelity."

index

Page numbers in **boldface** refer to photographs and illustrations.